POTTERS

Edited by Emmanuel Cooper and Eileen Lewenstein

An illustrated directory of the work of Fellows and Professional Members of the Craft Potters Association of Great Britain

A guide to visiting potters in their workshops

Educational sources for studying pottery in the United Kingdom

Eleventh Edition

Individual entries in the directory have been supplied
by the potters concerned

Edited by Emmanuel Cooper and Eileen Lewenstein
assisted by Daphne Matthews, Marilyn Kopkin and Julia Pitts

Cover — Felicity Aylieff, surface detail

Photographs supplied by individual potters or from Ceramic Review

Book design by Ceramic Review
.

Potters

First Edition	1972
Second Edition	1974
Third Edition	1975
Fourth Edition	1977
Fifth Edition	1980
Sixth Edition	1983
Seventh Edition	1986
Eighth Edition	1989
Ninth Edition	1992
Tenth Edition	1994
Eleventh Edition	1997

ISBN 0 9523576 1 5

Published by Ceramic Review Publishing Ltd.
21 Carnaby Street, London W1V 1PH

Contents

Introduction

'Potters' is the illustrated directory of the current work of Fellows and Professional Members of the Craft Potters Association. Earlier editions have proved to be useful guides to pots and potters in the United Kingdom and an invaluable source of information on work being made in the UK today. This, the eleventh edition, has been completely revised with new photographs of recent work, and up-to-date information on potters. Illustrations of potters at work reflect current interest in makers and their studios as well as the objects they make, and help to set the ceramic scene.

The first section gives an introduction to the Craft Potters Association. It briefly outlines its history, and the range of activities with which it is involved. The main part of the Directory consists of the listing of Fellows and Professional Members, between pages 9-288 in their alphabetical order. Following on the success of the use of colour, this new edition has even more colour illustrations, over 95% of the Fellows and Professional Members choosing to show their work this way. The result is a far more attractive and useful guide. Biographical notes are supplied by the potters themselves, and photographs illustrate recent work. Workshop and individual potters marks are included as an aid to identification. The directory gives a sound indication of work that is being made today, showing the range and diversity of contemporary ceramics, and it also serves as a useful record for future reference.

In the section 'Visiting a Potter' (pages 289-315), names, addresses and telephone numbers of members of the Craft Potters Association of Great Britain are listed together with details of visiting times, showroom opening and so on – invaluable information for anyone planning a visit. Some potters welcome callers to their showrooms and studios and some allow visitors to their showrooms only. This information is clearly stated together with the opening hours. Many of the potters have indicated that they welcome visitors, but by appointment only. If you wish to visit a potter who can only see you by appointment please write or telephone beforehand. A specially drawn map shows where workshops and studios open to the public are situated, but please check opening times before starting your journey.

'Working With Clay' is a valuable guide to a wide range of learning opportunities. It lists degree and vocational courses available at art schools, colleges and institutions of higher education and has been completely revised for this edition. It also contains information on part-time study. There is also useful advice on how to apply to work with potters in their workshops. A final section lists the recent meetings and activities of the Craft Potters Association.

The Craft Potters Association is the largest organisation of studio potters in Britain and has159 Fellows and 147 Professional Members. We are sure that this new edition will prove as useful a guide to contemporary ceramics in the United Kingdom as the previous ones. Every effort has been made to ensure that the information is correct at the time of printing.

The Craft Potters Association

The Association was formed as the Craftsmen Potters Association (CPA) in 1958 as a co-operative to sell the work of its potter members and to increase general awareness of the craft. In 1955 purchase tax had been extended to include domestic ware. This led Walter Lipton who was then at the Rural Industries Bureau to arrange an exhibition of pottery for export in a move to help potters; it was bought complete by a New Zealand store. This success prompted a group of potters to set up a working party to consider ways and means of forming an association that could organise similar activities.

Under the guidance of Walter Lipton the Craftsmen Potters Association was formed as an Industrial and Provident Society – Rosemary Wren was elected the first chairman and David Canter was appointed Honorary Secretary. The organisation is democratic; upon election each Fellow and Professional Member buys a £1 share and is entitled to elect Council Members and to vote at the Annual General Meeting. Policy decisions are made at Council Meetings when ideas from members are discussed.

The CPA is looking forward to the Millennium with over forty years experience behind it, and with confidence in the future of the craft. Recent changes in the administration and structure of the association have brought it more into line with current practice. In the first instance all members are elected, and are known as Professional Members. The category of Fellow was introduced to acknowledge experience and status, and as part of an intention to open up the membership of the Association to a wider range of potters, while the far-ranging and inventive activities of the Associates have taken membership to an impressive 800.

The establishment of The Craft Pottery Charitable Trust to further the educational aspects of the Association is a recognition of the importance of this work and the continuing need to educate and interest the public in the craft and to make information available to all potters. Equally useful has been the setting up of two trading companies, one dealing with the retail activities of Contemporary Ceramics, the other with Ceramic Review Publishing. All is under the watchful eye of the elected Council of the Craft Potters Association, the potters who give their time and energy to maintaining the democratic and fair basis on which the CPA was founded – a noble intent whereby the CPA continues to be owned and controlled by its elected members.

Contemporary Ceramics

The Council decided early on to open a shop, then known as the Craftsmen Potters Shop, to sell the work of its members in the heart of London's West End. In the Spring of 1959 a lease was taken on premises in Lowndes Court, Carnaby Street before the street gained its present fame. The interior of the shop and basement was built by a team of volunteers who worked in their free time for the following twelve months. On May 30th 1960 the shop opened with a superb exhibition of Ray Finch's stoneware.

In March 1966 the Association acquired larger shop premises in a building being erected in Marshall Street on the site of the house where William Blake was born. David Attenborough performed the opening ceremony of the new shop on December 4th 1967.

In 1988 the rear part of the shop was converted into a gallery and named after David Canter to commemorate the work and achievement of the Association's first Honorary Secretary. Major exhibitions by established members of the CPA and shows by potters at the start of their career are held in the gallery. The shop also contains a 'Collector's Cabinet' of work by early studio potters such as Bernard Leach, Michael Cardew, Katharine Pleydell-Bouverie and Denise Wren, all one-time members of the CPA, whose work is now finding a new and appreciative audience. 'Contemporary Ceramics' is unique in Central London selling and exhibiting only studio pots. The shop also has a well equipped sundries section which stocks sponges, turning tools, cane handles, Chinese brushes, wires etc. all at very competitive prices. A wide range of books on ceramics as well as international catalogues and magazines on pottery are on sale in addition to postcards of specially photographed pots. Fellows, Professional Members, Associate and Student Members are entitled to a 10% discount on all purchases except books.

In 1990 the shop adopted the new name *Contemporary Ceramics, the Craft Potters Shop and Gallery*. Improvements to the interior display continue to be made, including an enlarged Books section showing a large selection of current titles – an excellent place to browse and make new discoveries. Further exciting developments occurred in 1997 with the award of £100,000 Lottery Grant to enable the Council to re-design the shop premises. This enabled adequate provision for disabled people, and has created a fresh, open and bright setting for some of the finest ceramics in the country.

CPA Membership

The CPA is the only national body representing studio potters. Fellows and Professional Members are elected by the Council and all have full voting rights. Fellows are entitled to show their work in Contemporary Ceramics. Professional Members may be invited to show their work and to take part in special exhibitions. Associate membership is open to anyone interested in ceramics. Many Associates live overseas. All Fellows, Professional Members and Associates receive a copy of the bi-monthly newsletter CPA News with advance information of all events, priority booking, reduced fees, exhibition invitations and a discount on the purchase of pots from Contemporary Ceramics. The Association encourages the involvement of younger potters and in 1996 a student membership category was introduced. For information about CPA membership contact: The Membership Secretary, Craft Potters Association of Great Britain, 21 Carnaby Street, London W1V 1PH. Telephone 0171 437 6781 Fax 0171 287 9954.

Association Activities

As well as 159 Fellows and 147 Professional Members, the Craft Potters Association has an average of 800 Associate Members who contribute much to its activities. Many of the association's activities are the responsibility of council sub-committees including the Members and Associates Advisory Committee. CPA Archives are under the care of Moira Vincentelli at Aberystwyth Arts Centre (University College of Wales). Evening meetings have included talks by eminent potters from both this country and overseas. Recent talks have been given by, amongst others, Alison Britton who discussed developments in her work. Weekend events are arranged from time to time, the most recent of which was the highly successful Kiln Building Demonstration and talk with Ben Casson in May 1997. Publication is also well established of a regular newsletter for all members CPA News . This carries news of shop and association activities, a letters section plus articles by members. Associate members receive advance information of all events, priority booking, reduced fees and invitations to private views of exhibitions.

Ceramic Review Publications

The internationally acclaimed magazine Ceramic Review, a contemporary survey of studio pottery, is published by Ceramic Review Publications Ltd. The 60-page magazine appears six times a year and has extensive circulation both in this country and abroad. Members can subscribe to the magazine at a reduced rate. Other publications are The Ceramic Review Book of Clay Bodies and Glaze Recipes (4th edition 1988) which includes over 700 recipes from professional potters and has much useful advice on mixing and using bodies and glazes. Potters Tips edited by Robert Fournier, brought together the many useful tips published in Ceramic Review over the last 20 years and was published in 1990. A new publication A Guide to Public Collections of Studio Pottery in the British Isles compiled by Robert and Sheila Fournier has proved invaluable listing studio ceramics in public collections. Fully cross-indexed, the book is an essential reference for collections and museums.

Illustrated Directory of
CPA Fellows and Professional Members

**Most Fellows of the Association have work on sale at
Contemporary Ceramics the Craft Potters Shop. A full
list of Fellows and Professional Members together with
their addresses, can be found on page 289**

Lead Release

The Craft Potters Association is fully aware of the possible danger to health of
cadmium or lead released from glazed pottery into food. The CPA Council requires
all members sending work to the shop to state whether lead or cadmium are used in
their pottery or not. If these materials are present then potters must have their work
tested regularly and produce certificates to show that it conforms to the new
British Standard **BS6748**. The public can buy safely from the CPA shop.

Adrian Abberley Fellow

Adrian Abberley was born in Lancashire where he trained at a local art school until National Service which took him to Singapore for two years, where Buddhist temple architecture, Chinese theatre and the new environment were to provide a strong influence on future work. On returning to England he worked at Sadler's Wells Theatre until getting a job at Briglin Pottery. Since then he has had studios around London, one sharing with Guyanese potter Laurie Taitt and the Latvian potter Marga Slega. At present he is working in Richmond making stoneware and porcelain in an electric kiln using a glaze that resembles raku with on-glaze and lustre decoration. He also paints and has exhibited in various galleries.

Billy Adams Fellow

Billy Adams

Billy Adams My cultural identity, immediate surroundings and the landscape strongly influence my work. I consider this association, and an experiment with form, texture, materials and colour evident in the vessels. I produce this effect by handbuilding a pot, usually from a thrown base, working upwards in several stages. I use three different sorts of clay. First, an interior layer of craft crank. Next, an intermediate layer of clay mixed to prevent shrinkage of the pot during firing. Last, an outer surface of porcelain that is encouraged to buckle and crack as I shape the form from inside the pot. Thus the porcelain retains a fine hard texture, rather than becoming friable. At the midway stage I introduce a stylistically intrusive form such as a regular circular thrown handle or a smoothed rim - to represent the intervention of humans in the natural world.

David Allnatt

Allnatt

David Allnatt Born in London, studied graphics at Sutton School of Art, Surrey, in the sixties.
I make a range of non-functional vessels mostly fired to 1260°C in an electric kiln. All of the work is handbuilt using a grogged white stoneware body. Inspiration for the forms, colours and textures I use comes from observation of the landscape and an interest in surfaces that have been weathered and eroded. Work has been included in many exhibitions and is housed in both public and private collections.

Marilyn Andreetti

Marilyn Andreetti I trained at Farnham School of Art 1966-69, and taught art and design for ten years before deciding to work at home. I now work from a small converted coach house which overlooks my garden. I make some individual architectural pieces, but most of my current work is brightly coloured earthenware plates, jugs, bowls and clocks which I throw or handbuild in slabs using red clay. I decorate with underglaze colours and oxides on a white slip and finish with sgraffito. I fire bisque to 1040°C and then fire to 1080°C using a clear glaze in an electric kiln. I enjoy making colourful, decorative, commemorative yet functional ware. I sell through exhibitions, craft fairs and from the workshop.

Tim Andrews Fellow

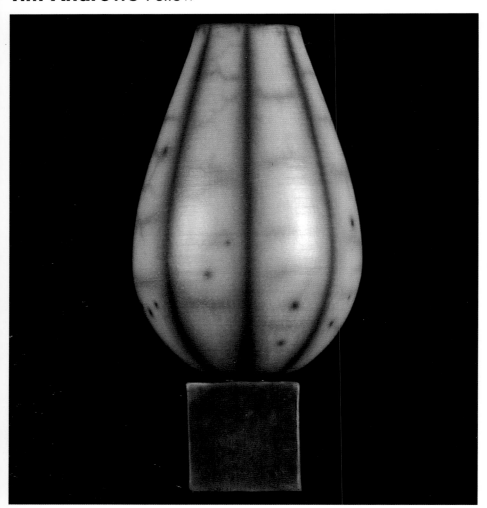

Tim Andrews Burnished and smoked pots including raku. Recent work has seen a move to larger pieces and more sculptural forms - although my vessel-orientated background is never very far away. Shapes have evolved with the use of linear decoration and subtle coloured slips which are further muted by the smokey firing. Trained with David Leach and at Dartington 1978-81. Set up workshop in Exeter then South Tawton 1981-86. Now working from own house and workshop in East Devon. Work is exhibited widely in the U.K. and in Europe. Author of *Raku - A Review of Contemporary Work*, A & C Black.

Mick Arnup Fellow

Arnup.

Mick Arnup has a fine arts background completing his training at the Royal College of Art in 1953. In 1972, after a stint of teaching at York School of Art, he became a full time potter using a 70cu.ft. oil fired kiln to make a range of reduced decorated stoneware, large garden pots, architectural ceramics, numerals and letters. He exhibits regularly in the U.K. and abroad, often with his wife, the animal sculptor, Sally Arnup, with whom he shares workshops and a showroom at Holtby.

Keith Ashley Fellow

Keith Ashley Born Yeovil, Somerset, 1944. Trained at Farnham Art College 1962-65. Studios in Somerset, Hampshire and London 1965-95. 1995 - in conjunction with Chris Barnes established The Chocolate Factory in Stoke Newington, London N16, to accommodate potters and other artists and craftspeople. Produces raku-fired sculpture.

Chris Aston Fellow

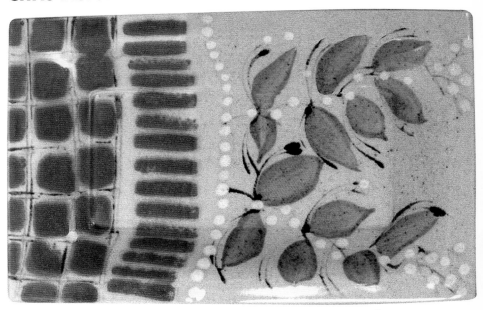

Chris Aston Chris celebrates 30 years as a full time potter in 1997, and is currently exploring several new directions. His interest in computer graphics is leading to a series of designs and glaze decoration based on computer images, with Kai's Power Tool filters applied to hand rendered images in the Photoshop programme, as the main source of inspiration. These, combined and interpreted with glaze on press-moulded and thrown forms, will provide the basis of future ceramic and glass exhibitions in conjunction with his son Dan, a hot glass artist who works nearby. With the close similarities between ceramic glaze and glass, many reflected themes and ideas will result. Chris's current range also includes his easily recognisable and favourite copper red halo and brushwork decoration.

Felicity Aylieff Fellow

F. Aylieff.

Felicity Aylieff Traditional hand-forming and plaster mould-making techniques are adapted to produce sculptural forms on an architectural scale. The work is constructed using a composite clay mix (recently researched at the RCA) that has in its make-up aggregates of glass and coloured porcelains. When ground and polished, the surfaces of this ceramic terrazzo are exotically tactile and rich in visual texture. I continue to produce vessels of a domestic scale which explore archetypal form. These are made using coloured clays and decorated with inlaid agate and slips. I exhibit extensively throughout Britain and abroad, and lecture full-time on the degree course at Bath College.

Elizabeth Aylmer

Elizabeth Aylmer I regard myself as self-taught but in fact was generously instructed by a friend who had not only been to art college but also served a rigorous apprenticeship at Denby with the original classical throwers, thus for many years speed and precision were my goals. This was a good discipline and enabled me to produce large quantities of ware at reasonable prices. Having been raised in Zimbabwe my influences are drawn from African culture and this is instantly recognisable both in my domestic ware and the individual pots that I make when time allows.

Duncan Ayscough

Duncan Ayscough After studying 3D Design in Manchester and subsequently a Masters Degree in ceramics at Cardiff, I have now established my studio in the Brecon National Park. In addition to my studio concerns I also lecture in a number of colleges. My work is primarily a reflection of my love of the making process. The movement of form and structure provided by the potters wheel is endlessly intriguing. All pots are one-off pieces, thrown and turned. Surfaces are constructed using terra-sigillata, occasionally employing surface carbonisation techniques. All work is polished with wax and additions of gold leaf are occasionally made.

Sylph Baier

Sylph Baier Trained in Germany and West Wales. Attended Dyfed College of Art 1981-84 and is currently working in Brighton as part of a mixed-disciplined group studio. Produces various ranges of domestic ware using slips, sgraffito and majolica techniques.

Chris Barnes

Chris Barnes Studied sculpture at St. Martins School of Art 1979-82. Discovered pottery at Islington Adult Education Institute and has worked with clay since 1987. In 1995 set up present workshop at The Chocolate Factory Studios in Hackney. The distinctive design and decoration of his reduced stoneware is a response to diverse influences, not least the desire to make something that people want to use at a reasonable cost. An empathy for the nature of the making process itself and the generosity and breadth of treatment felt in certain peasant wares is given contemporary sensiblity in his functional pots.

Richard Baxter

Richard Baxter I was born in 1959 and studied ceramics at Loughborough College of Art finishing in 1981 with a First. I established my first studio with a Crafts Council Setting Up Grant. I now have a well-lit studio and gallery in Old Leigh with splendid views over the Thames Estuary. Most of my output is domestic earthenware decorated with vitreous black and white slips and partially glazed giving strong contrasts of colour and texture. I fire to 1074°C in my electric top loading kiln. My one-off pieces I call 'relics' and are reminiscent of broken and restored archaeological finds.

Svend Bayer Fellow

Svend Bayer makes wood-fired stoneware garden pots and domestic pots. These are influenced by rural France, provincial Chinese and early American stoneware, and are fired in a large wood-fired cross-draught, single chamber kiln of some 800 cu.ft. Mostly the pots rely on fly ash, although the insides of domestic pots are glazed and all the bowls, plates and dishes are glazed and decorated.

Deborah Baynes

Deborah Baynes I am probably better known for my residential summer workshops, which I have held every year since 1971, originally at White Roding in Essex and since 1993 from Nether Hall, which overlooks the estuary of the River Orwell in Suffolk. However, between courses I have always produced a great many pots. My constant preoccupation has been with throwing and the endless variations, possibilities and pleasure to be had from manipulating wet clay both on and off the wheel - combined of course with the alchemy of fire. Since 1986 my work has been almost entirely saltglazed except (as I have always done) for periods spent making raku for the sheer fun of it. In 1997 I had a video made of my throwing techniques. My work is available through various exhibitions and from my workshop. I am a founder member and chairperson of The East Anglian Potters Association, a member of the Suffolk Craft Society and on the Craft Potters Association Professional and Associates Advisory Committee.

Peter Beard Fellow

Peter Beard makes thrown and handbuilt individual pieces in stoneware. The work is vessel and non-vessel based using glazes built-up in multiple layers with wax as a resist between the layers to create pattern and texture. High and low temperature glazes with coloured pigments are used to achieve matt and fluid textures giving a wide range of pastel to strong colours. Exhibits in solo and mixed exhibitions in many countries. His work is represented in many public and private collections. Regularly gives lectures and demonstrations and has done workshop tours of Austrailia and New Zealand. Awarded various grants and scholarships for research and travel. Author of *Resist and Masking Techniques*, published by A & C Black. Winner of the 1996 Inax design prize from Japan.

John Bedding

John Bedding Worked throughout the seventies at the Leach Pottery, interrupted by a year in France. In 1979 was invited by Shigeyoshi Ichino to study at his family's pottery in Tampa, Japan. On his return he set up his own workshop and now makes raku-fired individual pieces. Most are wheel-thrown with burnished and textured surfaces. Some are raku-fired with silver nitrate and copper glaze decor, others are fumed with metallic salts. A full range of his work can be seen in the St. Ives Pottery Gallery which adjoins his workshop in the centre of St. Ives.

Beverley Bell-Hughes Fellow

Beverley Bell-Hughes Born Epsom 1948. Trained at Sutton School of Art 1965-67, Harrow Studio Pottery Course under Victor Margrie and Michael Casson 1967-69. Work has been exhibited abroad and at home. My work is handbuilt, the shapes governed by both the making process and my interest in natural forms and growth. My aim is to get across the feeling of the material, clay, creating a bond with natural forms and being aware of the identity of the pot as a usable container if need be. I do not set out to imitate nature, but aspire to echo the process of nature.

Terry Bell-Hughes Fellow

Terry Bell-Hughes Trained at Harrow School of Art 1967 under Victor Margrie and Michael Casson. Primarily interested in high fired domestic pots thrown in series reflecting influences from Oriental and British country pots. Exhibited in several solo and many shared exhibitions in Britain and abroad. Work included in several public and private collections.

Julian Bellmont

Julian Bellmont opened the High Street Pottery in November 1993 after spending 13 years at the Aldermaston Pottery. Julian believes his pots should give the user a happy feeling when using them, so they are colourful, lustrous and extremely durable. The pots are made of a fine stoneware so they are practical, durable and aesthetic. In the showroom there is a good range of domestic ware and decorative ware. Commissions are also undertaken to individual requirements.

Kochevet Ben-David Fellow

K. BenDavid.

Kochevet Ben-David was born in Israel and having completed a BA in History of Art and English Literature at the Hebrew University came to England to study ceramics. Her deep interest in functional domestic ware was 'fired' at Harrow on the HND Ceramic Design course. She works with Limoges porcelain which provides a resonant background for her brushed and trailed coloured slip decoration. In her work she aims to achieve Philip Rawson's ideal and make pots which are unequivocally utilitarian whilst also expressive, beautiful and delightful to use. To promote this concept she writes about ceramics and recently collaborated with Primavera (Cambridge) in curating the exhibition 'Dining Rites". Her work is sold in shops and galleries throughout the U.K.

Suzanne Bergne Fellow

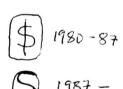

1980-87

1987 —

Suzanne Bergne studied literature and philosophy at Munich and Vienna universities (1958-63). She then lived and worked for some years in the Middle East. 1977-80 she trained as a potter at Croydon School for Art and Design. Afterwards, she worked and taught as a potter in Greece and Hong Kong. In 1987 she settled in England. She is known for her porcelain bowls and tall beakers decorated with poured glazefields either in rich colours or forming dramatic fields of texture. Recently she has been involved with figurative sculpture. Her pots can be found in many private collections in Europe, USA and Japan, and in the Victoria and Albert Museum, the Hong Kong Museum of Art, and the Hong Kong Tea Museum.

Maggie Angus Berkowitz Fellow

Maggie Angus Berkowitz (signature)

Maggie Angus Berkowitz I make pictures with glazes on tiles. Work is usually commissioned, often figurative, and always personally designed for a specific site. I enjoy discussing work with clients. Work installed since the 10th Edition includes; M,J,X and Z with plants and animals' - portrait panels on 17"porcelain tiles for private swimming pool (detail illustrated); 'Road to Jerusalem' - 30m. circular labyrinth, Low Furness Primary School, black and white pavers with glazed quarry tile 'city'; Public toilet signage, Carnforth , Lancs.; Foyer Panel, Appleby War Memorial; Swimming Pool (seen in progress in photo.) 'Family Floor' with portraits of D&L Kindersley; Domestic panels for clients in UK, USA and Japan. Previous work for hospitals, schools, offices, leisure centres, gardens conservatories, Aga-backs and bathrooms have included memorials, games and heraldry. I use oxides, engobes and earthenware glazes on (usually) industrially produced blanks and floor tiles. Trained, taught, worked UK, Italy, Tanzania, USA, Japan. Exhibits when invited, and with 'Artists Working to Commission'.

John Berry Fellow

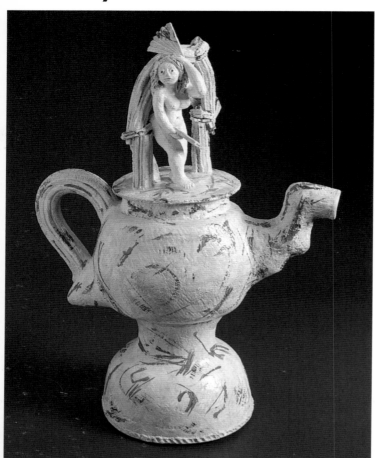

JOHN BERRY

John Berry Studied Architecture at the University of Westminster, Painting at Central St. Martins and ceramics at Wimbledon School of Art. Since 1986 lives and works in London and France. Work, including prints and drawings, in the collections of the Tate Gallery, Victoria and Albert Museum, Imperial War Museum, Welsh Arts Council, Bramah Tea and Coffee Museum, KLM (Holland),Museum Sztuki Poland, Hope College and Wooster Art Museums, USA. My pots are handbuilt individual pieces, usually relating to and including the figure, decorated with coloured glazes and lustres on white and buff stoneware.

David Binns

David Binns I originally trained at Manchester Polytechnic. I am currently Senior Lecturer in Ceramics and 3 D Design at the University of Lancashire in Preston and have a studio at home in North Wales. I make one-off ceramic forms that are the product of many influences and interests including: a fascination with numerical and mathematical pattern and repetition (that orders much of our lives), an interest in the notions of function and ambiguity and most importantly the joy of working clay itself. The majority of my current work is constructed from pierced or marked clay slabs. I do however hold no particular allegiance to any single making process - ultimately I enjoy the process of creating and solving problems!

Keith Booth

KB

Keith Booth After studying ceramics at Hornsey College of Art, he set up his first workshop in London in 1975 and then moved to Maidstone in 1981. He enjoys using a variety of forming techniques and manipulating texture, form and glaze finish to create his distinctive individually produced pieces. He works mainly with oxidised stoneware firing to 1260°C. His work is in collections in the UK and overseas.

Martin Booth

Martin Booth My pieces are based upon ideas from the landscape, particularly from around the Peak District and the area where I live. Common themes run throughout many of the works, for example contours from an horizon, opposites - sharp and smooth, light and dark, straight and curved. Forms develop in an organic way, growing, swelling and finally enclosed at the top. Work grows freely, allowing changes and developments to take place throughout the making process, often transforming the work considerably from the original idea. Work is constructed with a coarse stoneware clay, using combinations of slabs and coils. All works are stoneware fired.

Richard Boswell

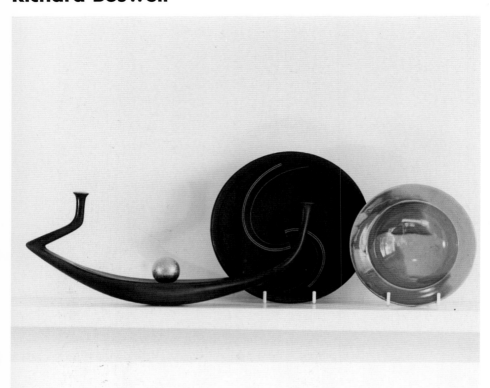

Richard Boswell has moved from his workshop by Emsworth Mill Pond to a riverside workshop at home. "The precisely inlaid earthenware bowls, for which I am mainly known, continue to evolve as new designs and colours are developed." Recent experiments with this earthenware body have led to both collections of jewellery which combine fine vitrified clay extrusions and carvings with gold, and more sculptural pieces which are ground and polished to a fine surface and often involve the use of lustres and gold leaf. The occasional recreational excursions into gas-fired stoneware helps me to keep a grip on reality.

Clive Bowen Fellow

Clive Bowen The pottery was established in 1971. The pots are thrown in red earthenware clay and range from large-scale store jars and garden pots to mugs and egg cups. The domestic ware and one-off pots may be decorated with contrasting slips using slip trailing, combing and sgraffito methods. His pots are once-fired in a round (8' dia.) down-draught wood-fired kiln to 1040°C-1060°C (less for garden pots).

Loretta Braganza Fellow

Braganza

Loretta Braganza trained in Graphics with a fine arts background. Makes handbuilt flattened vessel forms. The pots are evolved around three main concepts: forms, related shapes and colour. The textured slipware is a constantly evolving technique using a combination of coloured clay, and underglaze colours. Work in public, corporate and private collections in Britain and abroad.

Carlo Briscoe and Edward Dunn Fellows

REPTILE
tiles & ceramics

Carlo Briscoe and Edward Dunn have worked full-time under the name 'Reptile' since 1988. Make large tile panels for private and commercial clients including Waitrose Supermarkets. Also produce a range of mirrors, wall-plaques and ceramics which are sold through shops and galleries throughout the UK and abroad. The work is all tin-glazed earthenware and decoration is both painted and in relief. Recently moved from London to rural West Wales to a former butter factory.

David Brown

David Brown I continue to explore the teapot, both as a functional object, and as a vehicle for the expression of ideas. The possibilities seem endless. Vases and jugs have been subjected to the same exploration, influenced by visits to the Heraklion Archaeological Museum. I also make a range of, mostly thrown, stoneware pots, and have recently been involved with bowl forms, which allow for the experimentation of a variety of subtle glaze variations.

Sandy Brown Fellow

Sandy Brown Trained in Daisei pottery, Mashiko, Japan. Widely exhibited in the UK, Japan, Austrailia and Europe. Runs courses on 'Letting Go'. Makes expressive lively pots showing the tactile sensuality of soft clay and fresh spontaneous decoration. And clay figures, some life-size, which are intuitive; currently womanly, sexual, spiritual.

Jenny Browne

Jenny Browne I am very much a thrown-form potter and because my designs are very curvaceous I prefer generous round surfaces to work on or platters and bowls which I can decorate inside if they are shallow and wide, or on the outside if they have height. I enjoy knowing that my pots are usable for tableware and not just decorative. My favourite method of decoration is laborious as I combine painting on slip and sgraffito, often removing areas of slip to enable me to add other colours. I find it very satisfying as I achieve a strong hard-edge design. I am using white stoneware clay with an egg-shell finish white glaze, not highly reflective, which suits my work and I fire to 1220°C. As I have New Zealand roots my pots have a South Pacific influence no matter how hard I try to get away from it!

Susan Bruce

Susan Bruce Studied ceramics at Cheltenham and at Lowestoft Colleges of Art, she taught art and ceramics in schools and colleges before setting up as a maker in 1987. Susan has always been interested in the forms of domestic pottery, teapots, jugs, coffee pots, bowls etc. and her work is based on these traditions. The inspiration for her designs comes from her study of bird and plant life. After bisque firing, underglaze colours are applied, selected areas are glazed with a transparent glaze. Then gold and coloured lustres are applied and the work is fired a third time before it is finally completed.

Karen Bunting

Karen Bunting has been working in East London since 1979 producing domestic ceramics in reduction fired stoneware. She produces a range of jugs, bowls and dishes. Her work is characterised by geometric surface decoration which enhances the form of each piece. She exhibits and sells work throughout the UK and abroad.

Jan Bunyan

Jan Bunyan I set up my workshop in 1980, fifteen years after gaining a degree in French Studies, Since then I have worked full-time as a potter making domestic pottery using red earthenware, slips and colour. My work can be seen in various galleries including Traffords in Stow-on-the-Wold and Art-in-Action gallery at Waterperry, as well as at the Gloucestershire Guild of Craftsmen.

Deirdre Burnett Fellow

DB

Deirdre Burnett studied sculpture at St. Martins School of Art and then took a BA in Ceramics at Camberwell School of Art. Set up first workshop in Dulwich, mainly producing tableware. Now makes individual pieces in oxidised stoneware and porcelain, usually vessel forms. They are wheel thrown, turned and altered. Has exhibited widely. Work in many private and public collections including Museum of Modern Art, New York; the Victoria and Albert Museum, London; Boymans van Beuningen Museum, Rotterdamm; the National Gallery of Victoria, Melbourne, Australia. On the Crafts Council Selected Index.

Ian Byers Fellow

Ian Byers The preoccupations of my work are both poetic and sculptural, often drawing together ideas and images to create mood and interplay. I am interested in harmony and conflict, easiness and unease, sometimes contained in the same piece. Recently I have undertaken commission work some of which included surface pattern designs for tableware. Most of the sculptural work is low fired, sometimes smoked. Ian Byers is the author of *Raku*, part of the *Complete Potter* series published by Batsford, he teaches at Bath College of Higher Education on the BA Hons.Ceramics course and also at colleges in Sweden. He has exhibited in England, Europe and the USA and has work in collections in Britain and Europe.

John Calver Fellow

Calver

John Calver I was twenty-two when captivated by my first contact with clay. Four years later I gave up my civil engineering career to pot full-time. Initially I made domestic earthenware but, seduced by high temperature glazes, I changed to reduced stoneware. My forms are all thrown on the wheel and remain functional but have become progressively more highly decorated. The surface may be textured with fabric, clay stamps, rope or chattering; slips are brushed, sponged, trailed or inlaid; and finally, after biscuit firing, up to seven glazes are poured in partly overlapping layers.

Kyra Cane

Kyra Cane signature

Kyra Cane was born in 1962 in Southwell, Nottinghamshire and studied ceramics at Camberwell School of Art between 1982 and 1985. She received a Crafts Council Grant in 1987 and has exhibited widely since then. Her time is divided between her workshop in Mansfield and teaching on the BA Hons. degree in ceramics at Harrow, University of Westminster where she is a principal member of the course team. Bowls and jugs are recurrent themes in her work and she makes pieces in series being constantly engaged by subtle variations in each form. Pots are thrown on a wheel in one or two parts and glaze fired to1285°C; lightly reduced in a gas kiln. The interplay of form and surface are an important element of her work and she applies layers of oxide, stain and glaze until the surface is animated by a series of marks, some textured and gritty, others with areas of rich turquoise and green that have references which are distilled from her observations of landscape.

Seth Cardew Fellow

Seth Cardew makes wood-fired stoneware pots that are useful and decorative. The Wenford Bridge Pottery is run in an outward and forward-looking style, and has been in existence for fifty-eight years. A collection of pots reflecting this history is open to visitors. A brochure for residential courses on wheel-made pots is available on request.

Daphne Carnegy Fellow

Daphne Carnegy studied pottery as an apprentice to a faience potter in France and subsequently at the Harrow Studio Pottery course. Since 1980 she has had her own workshop in London, producing thrown and painted tin-glazed earthenware in the maiolica tradition. She aims to combine the highly decorative, exhilarating qualities of maiolica with functional pottery for everyday use - the forms, colours and patterns all intended to enhance enjoyment of food and drink. Fruit and sea designs are expressed in a bold Mediterranean palette but more recent abstract designs explore subtler tones. Daphne is also the author of *Tin-glazed Earthenware* published by A & C Black in 1993.

Tony Carter

Tony Carter

MADE IN
ENGLAND
©

Tony Carter studied ceramics at Bath Academy of Art 1971-74 (BA Hons) with post graduate year at Goldsmiths' College ATD. Started his own pottery with his wife Anita in 1978, specialising in slip cast work. Today the pottery has gained an international reputation for the collectable teapots made at the premises. Approximately 75% of its production is shipped worldwide. The pottery is based in the beautiful village of Debenham, set in the heart of Suffolk which is open to the public all year round, firsts and bargains available in the pottery shop, also viewing area, tea and coffee available in the courtyard, weather permitting.

Michael Casson Honarary Fellow

Michael Casson Early member of CPA 1957/58. Chairman early 1960s. Council member until early 1970s. Co-founder of Harrow studio pottery course 1963 (with Victor Margrie), founder board member of Dartington Pottery Training Workshop; 1983 OBE, 1985-88 Vice-Chairman of Crafts Council. Books: *Pottery in Britain Today*, 1966, *Craft of the Potter*, 1976 (Presenter of BBC TV series). First pots 1945. First workshop London 1952-59. Tin-glazed earthenware. Second workshop 1959-77 Buckinghamshire, full range of domestic stoneware with Sheila Casson. Present workshop wood and gas fired saltglaze, individual functional pots, jugs, jars, teapots, etc.

Sheila Casson Fellow

Sheila Casson In 1955 I shared a workshop with Michael Casson in London making tin-glazed earthenware fired in an electric kiln. Early member of CPA 1958. 1959 made functional oxidised stoneware, then reduction fired in a gas kiln. 1977 moved to Wobage Farm making individual porcelain bowls with decoration inspired by the Herefordshire landscape. Since 1990 returned to functional ware in saltglaze, specifically teapots, jugs, vases and bowls. The teapots and jugs and vases are thrown and altered, and the bowls thrown with decorative handles and knobs. In 1997 making handbuilt pieces as well as thrown pots. All of these inspired by early Mediterranean pots. Work reduction fired in gas and wood kilns to 1300°C.

Trevor Chaplin

Trevor Chaplin Trained in architecture, then as a teacher, specialising in pottery and design (1970-73). After teaching for 17 years, I have been potting, full-time, for the past eight years. Now working in my purpose-built studio in the Wiltshire countryside producing thrown reduction stoneware. My pots are faceted, embossed, and textured to give the high fired ash and shino glazes a sense of movement as they roll, break and pool over the clay body. Slips are often applied and brushed through to expose the inherent characteristics and freshness of the clay beneath. Presently exploring soda vapour glazing over textured surfaces. All my pots are made to be used and enjoyed.

Richard Charters

Richard Charters Since graduating in 1982 with a degree in 3D Design from Farnham, I have worked in two of England's oldest potteries, making terracotta garden pots at Farnham Potteries, and coal-fired saltglaze gardenware at Bardon Mill, Northumberland. At Harehope, I make a range of gardenware and tiles from a local brick clay. All pots are thrown on a home-built momentum wheel, specifically designed for big-ware production, and fired with wood in a 170 cu.ft. cross-draught kiln, to 1000°C making the ware frost-proof. Commissions are welcome.

Linda Chew Fellow

CHEW.

Linda Chew graduated from Cheltenham College of Art in 1973 with a degree in sculpture, from the Institute of Education in 1975 with an Art Teacher's Certificate, and set up her workshop in 1975 while teaching in Winchester. Her ideas are influenced by a love of textiles, the movement within their patterns, plus a desire to produce pieces that appear soft and tactile. Shaped slabs of porcelain and T-material are impressed with lace, haberdashery, etc. and assembled. After a biscuit firing, patterns created are then embellished with oxides and underglaze colours over wax resist, and fired to 1260 °C in an electric kiln.

Derek Clarkson Fellow

                                    '97   '98   '99   2000
                                    DC   •▼   ••   ••   ■   year
                                                                symbols

Derek Clarkson has been potting for almost fifty years. CPA member from 1961/2 and began exhibiting. Lecturing in ceramics 1947-79. Full-time potting since 1980. During the 1980s gave lecture/ demonstrations for ceramic societies and Potterycrafts Ltd. Now enjoying working alone mainly using porcelain bodies making individual decorative bottles and bowls by throwing and turning. Wood ash and celadon glazes are used with cobalt and iron calligraphic brush decoration as well as tenmoku, titanium, kaki and copper reds. Some porcelain bowls have incised designs exploring graduations of translucency. These glazes are fired to 1300°C with reducion in a 12 cu. ft. gas kiln. Burnishing gold is frequently added. Zinc silicate crystalline glazes on porcelain have been produced since 1990 and now account for 50% of the work (see *Ceramic Review* 137, *The Studio Potter* Vol.25 No1 and *Contemporary Porcelain* by Peter Lane). Represented in many private collections and public galleries including the Victoria and Albert Museum, City Museum & Art Gallery, Stoke on Trent and the City Art Gallery, Manchester.

Margery Clinton Fellow

Margery Clinton studied painting at Glasgow School of Art. She began research into reduction lustres at the Royal College in 1973 and still continues this work. Author of *Lustres* (Batsford) 1991. Increasingly involved in architectural projects which she enjoys, and is particularly interested in tiles. Recent commissions have included a ceramic mural for The Mary Erskine School Edinburgh, new Glasgow 'wally closes' and the staff loos at the Scottish National Portrait Gallery, Edinburgh. Currently working on a commission for porcelain lights for a stairwell. Collections: Tate Gallery, Victoria and Albert Museum, Glasgow Art Gallery, Royal Museum of Scotland.

Peter Clough Fellow

Peter Clough I have been working as a ceramist both full and part-time for over thirty years. My principal formal concerns reside with notions of the vessel as object, with illusion and paradox, and as a vehicle for personal experience and biography. My recent work is largely assembled from textured slabs plus extrusions, and then raku fired with post-firing fuming with chlorides using a variety of fibre kilns. Contrasts of scale are a recent development, with some work over three feet high, and others in miniature combined with silver and gold. Recent solo and group exhibitions in the UK, Germany, and Switzerland. Currently Senior Lecturer at the University College of Ripon and York. St. John (York).

Desmond Clover

Desmond Clover My pots are thrown, some changed by cutting and adding rims and handles. I use a combination of abstracted and representational images and create depth within the surface of the vessel. I decorate with coloured glazes I have developed over the years. I like to build up the design like a painting, brushing, dipping and using wax resist, keeping it as fresh as possible. They are fired to 1280°C in a reduction atmosphere. I produce a variety of tableware but concentrate mainly on individual pieces. All my work is decorated with unique designs in stoneware and porcelain.

Russell Coates Fellow

Russell Coates I make underglaze blue enamelled porcelain, vases, jugs and shallow bowls mostly, which I decorate with seals, dolphins, whales, fish and sea creatures. I also do bird, deer and hare designs. I combine these images with various concentric circle, square and sunburst patterns. I start the decoration - dolphins, sunburst and geometric border for example, in underglaze blue on the biscuited shape which is then glazed and fired in reduction to 1270°C. The design is then completed in enamels and fired to 830°C, sometimes with gold. For years I worked with five enamel colours; red, yellow, green, blue and purple but now I have developed a sixth colour, a bright turquoise blue.

Rosemary Cochrane

Rosemary Cochrane I trained at Manchester Polytechnic. I have been making saltglazed stoneware pots over the past 15 years. It has been important that the pots I produced should be functional and also give pleasure as they are handled in preparing and serving food and displaying fruit and flowers. The wealth of traditional wares from Britain and Europe provide the influence for many of my ideas; for my domestic wares are created from the simplicity of form following function. The landscape and natural world around me inspire the colours with which I choose to work. The surfaces are decorated with an intuitive and free-spirited brush-work and trailed slips. They are enhanced by the rich qualities and varied effects of a salt-firing. My workshop is in the barn adjacent to the old farmhouse - set on a hillside in the Brecon Beacons National Park. I fire with gas in a 30 cu.ft. catenary arch kiln. I sell through craft galleries and exhibitions.

Roger Cockram Fellow

Roger Cockram Originally trained in science (zoology). Postgraduate work in marine ecology. Ceramics at Harrow 1973-75. Early work was wood-fired thrown ware. Recent work mainly individual pieces based on observed situations of marine and freshwater themes, often with added modelling and painting. Also makes a small range of ovenware, pitchers etc. All work is once-fired to cone 10-11 in a gas kiln and heavily reduced. Work sells through own showroom, galleries in UK and overseas; also through exhibitions and commissions.

Elaine Coles

Elaine Coles

Elaine Coles I make a wide range of reduced domestic stoneware, as well as some highly decorated one-off pieces, including large bowls and platters in bright colours freely applied with slip-trailers, stencils, sponges, etc. Originally I was self-taught, but in 1987 I spent a year at Goldsmiths' College on the Diploma Course where I concentrated on mould making and slipcasting, some of the techniques are incorpoated into my work. In 1993 I set up my present workshop. I bought an old Barclays Bank building in Chobham High Street and turned it into a galllery which is now a Crafts Council Selected Gallery and where my work is always on show together with other ceramics, textiles, wood, jewellery etc.

Nic Collins

Nic Collins set up his pottery at Powdermills near Postbridge, in the middle of Dartmoor, after leaving Derby College. He built a 60 cu.ft. wood-fired kiln from which he produces one-off pieces and a range of domestic ware. He sells these from his adjoining gallery, along with work from other craftspeople, artists and potters.

Barbara Colls Fellow

Barbara Colls Born in 1914. Attended West Surrey College of Art and Design part-time over many years. Paul and Penny Barron and Henry Hammond were a great help in developing the bird lidded pots in which I specialize. I work alone in tiny studio, using stoneware and porcelain, all my work is thrown and modelled using coloured slips and glazes. Exhibitions at many galleries at home and abroad.

Jennifer Colquitt

Jennifer Colquitt Qualifications - awarded First Class Honours in Ceramics from the University of Wolverhampton, 1974. My studio has been established in Dudley for several years. I make decorative wall panels, dishes, bowls and ceramic jewellery in high fired white or buff clay coloured with oxides and lustres. Currently my work is evolved from the combination of texture and fine detail. The themes used are many and varied, ranging from the observation of painting techniques such as pointillism to the study of patterns found in Eastern art.

Jo Connell

Jo Connell trained in ceramics at North Staffordshire Polytechnic, 1972, and combines running a workshop with teaching (currently Associate Lecturer at North Warwickshire and Hinkley College). I enjoy using a variety of processes - slabbing, coiling, throwing, press-moulding - often within the same piece. I work with coloured stoneware clays which are usually left unglazed, giving the piece a textile-like quality. My influences are wide ranging and my imagination is caught by situations where the juxtaposition of colours and textures create a pattern which I can interpret in clay. Techniques themselves tend to suggest new ways of working which continue to demand further experimentation.

Clare Conrad

Clare Conrad studied ceramics at Bristol, U.W.E. graduating in 1987. Her stoneware is distinctive for its painterly exploration of texture and colour, applied to the exterior surface of the finely thrown form. She makes mainly bowls and vases, which are sold in galleries throughout the UK and has work in private and public collections here and abroad.

Joanna Constantinidis Fellow

(photography - Tim Macpherson)
Joanna Constantinidis Individual pots in stoneware and porcelain, also some porcelain tableware.

Delan Cookson Fellow

Delan Cookson A characteristic, intense crystalline blue glaze is the most immediately attractive aspect of the ceramics of Delan Cookson. His forms - bowls, bottles and vases - invite touch as well as gaze. Since 1988, after a career in teaching, he has worked on his own in his Cornish studio, mostly in porcelain because of its delicate whiteness, which allows him to use both subtle and bright coloured glazes. Honoured by various awards, his ceramics are exhibited widely in collections in Britain and abroad.

Bennett Cooper Fellow

Bennett Cooper trained at Hornsey College of Art (Middlesex Polytechnic) 1971-74 and the Royal College of Art 1974-77. Set up present workshop in 1979. Working with high fired earthenware (1160°C). I produce a range of pressed and thrown highly decorative table and ovenware plus a few one-off pots and an increasing number of tile panels. Brightly coloured slips applied with trailer and brush enhanced with sgraffito and applied pigment enables me to work within the slipware tradition. The discipline involved in making decorative functional pots is a continual source of excitement and inspiration.

Emmanuel Cooper Fellow

Emmanuel Cooper Individual pots, mostly in porcelain, include bowls and jug forms. Glazes tend to be bright and rich and include turquoise blues and greens, nickel pinks and blues, uranium yellow. All are fired to 1260° C electric kiln. Has been making pots since 1965. Trained Dudley College of Education 1958-60, Bournemouth School of Art 1960-61, Hornsey School of Art 1961-62. Worked with Gwyn Hanssen and then Bryan Newman before opening own studio. Works alone. Co-editor (with Eileen Lewenstein) of *Ceramic Review* . Major exhibitions British Craft Centre, Boadicea, Craft Potters Shop, J.K. Hill, Beaux Arts, Bath, Ruthin Craft Centre, Contemporary Applied Arts. Work in many collections including Victoria and Albert Museum, Royal Scottish Museum. Author of many books on ceramics including *New Ceramics* (with Eileen Lewenstein), *Glazes for the Studio Potter* (with Derek Royle) (Batsford 1978), *The Potters Book of Glaze Recipes* (Batsford 1980), *A History of World Pottery* (Batsford 1988), *Electric Kiln Pottery* (Batsford 1982), *Cooper's Book of Glaze Recipes* (Batsford 1987), *Glazes* (Batsford 1992).

Gilles Le Corre Fellow

Gilles Le Corre trained at Camberwell School of Arts and Crafts 1975-79. Individual high fired stoneware pots.

Jane Cox

Jane Cox trained at Camberwell School of Art (1989-92) and at the Royal College of Art (1992-94) and now pots from her studio in Brockley, South London. She makes earthenware tableware using various techniques (throwing, casting, jolleying and handbuilding) and combines bold elegant forms with energetic, striking surface patterns. She uses a method of slip decoration whereby layers are elaborately built up upon one another and then enhanced through the use of coloured transparent glazes. Whilst making items that can be used every day, Jane's main interest is in making vessels which will transcend this, bringing beauty and meaning to our daily lives.

Louise Darby

Louise Darby In 1997 Louise Darby started her fourteenth year running her own studio, working in a converted farm building near Stratford-upon-Avon. She works on her own making finely thrown and turned stoneware and porcelain pots, altering and assembling some pieces, and developing new incised and carved designs, forms and glazes. An unexpected image on the underneath of a vase, or a shape that is actually pierced, show her continued attention to detail. Louise takes part in several exhibition a year, she also sells through some twenty galleries, and from her studio showroom, where visitors are very welcome by appointment.

Dartington Pottery Fellow

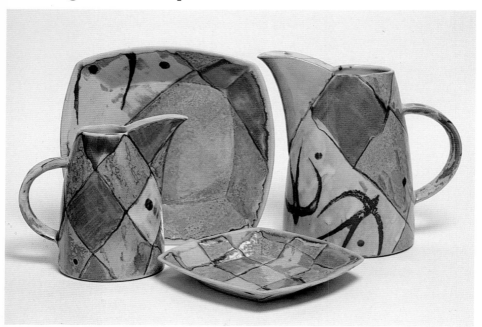

Dartington Pottery Dartington Pottery is located on the Dartington Hall Estate in South Devon. The original site was used by Bernard Leach and then by Marianne De Trey until 1981. Today the pottery is run by Stephen Course and Sue Cook employing up to 15 potters including positions for four apprentices. We specialise in reduction stoneware tableware and limited editions encouraging collaboration with outside designers as well as originating designs from within the workforce. These include Janice Tchalenko and Tavs Jorgensen. The pottery has its own shop on site and work is sold to specialist shops world wide. It is also included in public collections.

Joyce Davidson

Joyce Davidson I established the pottery in Castle Acre, Norfolk 9 years ago. All my work is thrown in stoneware or porcelain. Whilst surface decoration plays an important part in the finished work I also place great stress on the form of the vessel. I decorate using brushwork, fluting, wax resist and pigment/glaze reaction but sometimes rely on a simple celadon, ash or crackle glaze with perhaps a burnished metallic rim to emphasise and enhance the shape of the form. My work consists mainly of one-off pieces and I prefer not to specialise in one particular type of pot. For me, this would have the effect of narrowing my outlook and closing my eyes to new ideas. I tend instead to develop a theme and follow it through its various aspects to a point at which the next avenue of investigation opens up.

Richard Dewar

Richard Dewar

Richard Dewar First touched clay in 1954 at primary school and found it quite sticky. Just thumb pots then, baked in the sun. Painted and varnished. Then at big school in 1964. Earthenware and electric kiln. College at Corsham in 1966. Throwing, drinking and firing. College at Harrow in 1970, same but more intensive. Set up studio in Glos. in 1972 and had to learn it all over again. Moved to France in 1979. I've continued playing with clay, attempting to produce three or four good pots out of the hundreds I make each year. It's not easy!

Peter and Jill Dick Fellows

Peter and Jill Dick Coxwold pottery is a small country workshop established in 1965 by Peter and Jill Dick. Together they make a wide variety of kitchen/tableware, planters and commemorative pieces. At present the majority of work is earthenware, thrown and decorated with lively coloured slips. Peter, who was trained by Michael Cardew and Ray Finch, also makes limited numbers of platters and other large, more unusual pots for exhibitions and galleries. These are fired to low stoneware temperatures in the large wood burning kiln which gives a rich and exciting quality to glazes and bodies. Jill's more personal work is in stoneware, influenced by Eastern ceramics. Ash glazes, reduction fired in the gas kiln, have an austere beauty which contrasts with the lighter-hearted nature of the regular production. The village of Coxwold lies in famous countryside some 20 miles north of York. Visitors to the Pottery are welcome to look around the workshop (especially if they carry a copy of this book) and choose from the selection of pots in the showroom. In the Pottery Garden you will find a range of splendid plant pots from other English makers along with herbs and plants in season.

Mike Dodd Fellow

Mike Dodd ' Mike Dodd's pots are among the warmest and most immediate I know, and they need to be handled and used for their full qualities to be experienced; the depth of their character increasingly apparent as thay live longer around the house. I have an ash glazed jar, which has enviably assured turning at its base, free and strident, as if the pot is still turning on its wheel. This energy is compounded by fast but considered abstract engraving - crisp vertical and diagonal scouring which expresses the assured action of his hand, and the substance of the clay itself, forced out in channels by the potters tool. It is this sort of pot which evokes the whole cycle of making - the 'complete act' if you like - and also the sort of pot we look to for confirmation that the craft is alive and well; as Mike has put it "because of the heart, in spite of the head".
David Whiting 1996

Jack Doherty Fellow

Jack Doherty Porcelain, thrown with coloured clays then soda-fired. Work can be seen in the collections of the following museums; Ulster, Stoke-on-Trent, Liverpool, Cheltenham and the Keramiekmuseum het Princesshof, Leewarden, Holland. Currently chair of the Craft Potters Association.

Bridget Drakeford

Bridget Drakeford

Bridget Drakeford works alone making individual thrown porcelain. Simple classic shapes, sometimes carved and incised, with ash, celadon and copper glazes. Oxidised and reduction firings. Established since 1977 and exhibits widely in the UK and abroad.

John Dunn Fellow

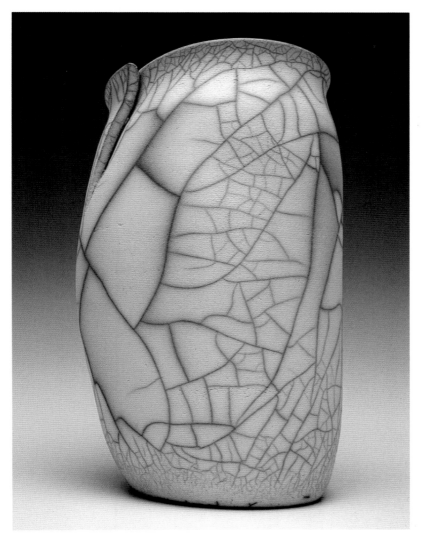

John Dunn I have for a number of years concentrated almost exclusively on the production of large raku dishes. Now I have decided to spend less time in this area to focus on one-off pieces using both raku and low fire techniques. Work is distributed throughout Europe and housed in both public and private collections. The workshop here in Brighton is becoming increasingly established as a training workshop offering intensive courses in both raku and low fire to individuals and groups. International demonstrations undertaken throughout Europe on location.

Geoffrey Eastop Fellow

Geoffrey Eastop trained as a painter at Goldsmiths' College, London and Academie Ranson, Paris. Over a long period has worked through a wide range of techniques. At present working in low-fired stoneware using hand-built and thrown techniques with surfaces textured and painted in vitreous slips. The emphasis is essentially on individual pieces. Currently making work for Germany and Japan. Exhibited widely in Britain and abroad. Architectural commissions include large murals for Maudsley Hospital, London; Reading Civic Centre Council Chamber and wall and floor tiles for Robinson College Chapel, Cambridge. Work in numerous public collections Victoria and Albert Museum, London, Fitzwilliam Museum, Cambridge; and National Museum of Wales. Book: The Hollow Vessel , Bohun Gallery 1980, Fellow Society of Designer-Craftsmen.

Victoria and Michael Eden

EDEN

Victoria and Michael Eden Working together we make slip decorated earthenware with a distinct European influence. Our present work is a search for bold, simple forms with a definite harmony of shape, strong colour and restrained decoration. We are also experimenting with clay bodies and the enhancement of glaze quality through wood-firing. The pottery produces a simple domestic range of cheerful pots for eating and drinking alongside individually designed one-off vessels. We supply many small shops and galleries throughout Britain (including Contemporary Ceramics, London) and have also designed and made ranges for Habitat in Britain and Barneys, USA and Japan.

Libby Edmondson

Libby Edmondson combined teaching with making and selling her own work for many years. She is now a full-time potter producing mainly animal forms and sometimes work which explores literary themes. She hand-builds with craft crank clay which is decorated with a variety of textural finishes, coloured slips and oxides.

Nigel Edmondson

Nigel Edmondson uses high fired grogged clay to make a range of garden ceramics and some decorative pieces. Much of the work incorporates architectural elements and reflects an interest in Islamic/Moorish decorative design. Surfaces are decorated with impressed patterns, coloured slips and oxide washes.

Derek Emms Fellow

Derek Emms Born 1929. Studied at Accrington, Burnley and Leeds Colleges of Art, taking National Diploma in Printed Textiles, and Ceramics (hand) and Teaching Certificate. After National Service in RAF worked at the Leach Pottery under Bernard and David Leach. From 1955 to 1985 full-time lecturer at North Staffs Polytechnic in Stoke-on -Trent. Retired in 1985 to devote more time to producing my own work. I produce a variety of domestic and 'one-off' pieces in stoneware and porcelain fired to 1280°C in a gas kiln. The pots are decorated by engraving in the leather-hard clay or by brush decoration on the biscuit with oxide pigments. Glazes include transparent, celadons, tenmoku, chun and copper red, and I enjoy experimenting with these glazes a) to give a better glaze fit and b) to open up awareness of expression.

James Evans

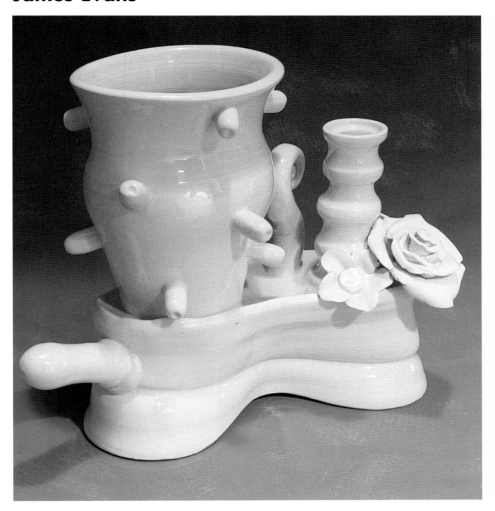

James Evans My interests in ceramics led me to study firstly at Central St. Martins College of Art and Design, London, and by way of a scholarship my MA at the University of Colorada, USA. On leaving college I held a couple of residencies, exhibited here in the UK, Germany, Denmark and the United States, and at present run my own studio and teach part-time. On the whole my work is sculptural, but I enjoy flirting with the practical side of ceramics.

Kirsti Buhler Fattorini

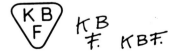

Kirsti Buhler Fattorini I was born in Winterthur, Switzerland being fortunate to be brought up in a community where the visual arts were highly regarded. On completing my formal education I went to Rome to study painting and ceramics. I made handbuilt earthenware pots decorated with bright abstract designs. On marrying and moving to England I was unable to find the materials I was used to and changed to stoneware thrown pots which I continue to decorate with abstract designs. More recently I have included slipcast stoneware dishes suitable for domestic use. I particularly enjoy decorating and experimenting with glazes. Currently my designs are drawn from nature - animals, birds, fish and flowers.

Dorothy Feibleman Fellow

Dorothy Feibleman makes laminated coloured porcelain and parian ceramics including 22 and 18 karat gold and porcelain jewellery. Her fascination with using lamination is that the structure and decoration are integral. She makes ceramics full-time and gives workshops and demonstrations. Her work is in many private and public collections including the Victoria and Albert Museum, the Indianapolis Art Museum, the Frankfurt, Darmstadt and Stuttgart Decorative Arts Museums.

Ray Finch Honorary Fellow

Ray Finch works with son Michael and team of three making wood-fired, thrown domestic stoneware for everyday use and some individual pots, as well as some personal saltglazed work.

Judith Fisher

Judith Fisher was born in Brighton. She studied Fine Art and Illustration at Brighton College of Art, followed by a year at Goldsmiths' College London, where she first became interested in ceramics. She specializes in making individual small-scale bowls and vases fired by the raku process in which the pot is withdrawn from the red-hot kiln to be plunged into sawdust or other organic matter. When the surface has been coated with powdered copper unpredictable colours from purple to turquoise and pink emerge. On other pieces bare clay receives interesting marks and veining from being fumed in stable sweepings.

Sylvia Des Fours Fellow

Sylvia Des Fours came to England from Czechoslavakia in 1949. Trained at Epsom and Hammersmith Schools of Art. Makes individual pieces in stoneware and porcelain, thrown with handbuilt extensions. At present researching 'Jade into Clay' experience and technique. Teaches at Surrey Heartlands, Epsom. Believes in the therapeutic value of working with clay and is deeply involved in matters of mental health.

David Frith Fellow

David Frith Born 1943, started his first workshop in 1963, first making earthenware slipware and porcelain. Work is thrown or extruded, mainly personal pieces and much on a large scale. Increased awareness of the materials has brought about continual development of his work. The milled celadons and iron glazes give rich qualities and heavy overglazes with wax resist, trailed glazes and pigments predominate. After 35 years or so potting, enthusiasm is just as strong as ever and he is currently developing work with extrusions including tiles and ceramic murals. The Brookhouse Pottery Schools are held each year. David gives lectures and workshops in this country and abroad. Past Council Member of the CPA, Index Member of the Crafts Council. Work in public and private collections.

Margaret Frith Fellow

Margaret Frith Born 1943, trained at Bolton, Liverpool and Stoke on Trent Colleges of Art. Started workshop with husband David Frith in 1963. Early work domestic ware production in earthenware and later reduction stoneware. Now making a range of personal work in stoneware and porcelain. Developed her own porcelain body which throws well and holds its shape. She carves into the body with free floral designs and covers with milled celadon glazes which flow into the carving. Work also includes coloured porcelain, currently bottles some with copper red glazes. Holds the Brookhouse Pottery Schools each year with David. Exhibits regularly in this country and abroad.

Tessa Fuchs Fellow

Tessa Fuchs Born Knutsford, Cheshire. Studied Salford Royal Technical College Art School, Central School of Arts and Crafts, London. Set up studio as an individual artist potter making sculptural pieces and some domestic ware in high fired earthenware using colourful matt glazes. Work inspired by animals, trees, plants, landscape, gardening, painting and sculpture. She is particularly influenced by her travels which have included China, Mexico, Africa and India. The work has an element of fantasy and humour. Her latest work is in the subect of the human form and most recently seascapes. She is now painting on a large scale as well as potting.

Liz Gale Fellow

Liz Gale Trained as a teacher, specialising in textile arts, she taught in infant schools for ten years. Self-taught as a potter, she divided her time between teaching and ceramics, becoming a full-time potter in 1988 and moving to her first purpose-built workshop and showroom in 1992. Specialising in domestic reduction stoneware, she uses a combination of latex, sponging, trailing and wax resist, to create decoration reminiscent of textile designs. She constructed her 30 cu.ft. dry-built kiln which is propane fired. Elected to the CPA Council and appointed Honorary Secretary in 1992.(Photography Nigel Rigden)

Tony Gant Fellow

Tony Gant makes stoneware bowls, dishes, plates, jugs, mugs and vases. Established 1961; present studio since 1968.

Philip Gardiner

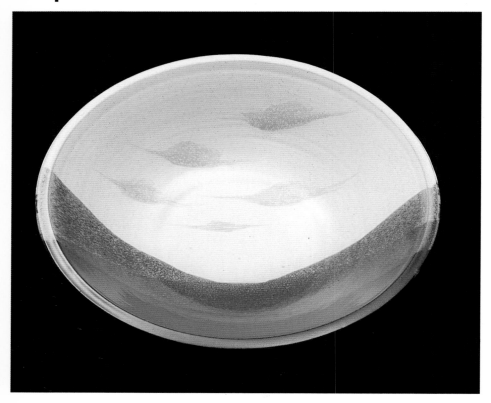

PG

Philip Gardiner I have been making pottery for over 25 years. Studying at North Staffordshire Polytechnic followed by time gaining experience at other potteries, including 8 years as a production thrower. In 1983 I set up my own pottery by the sea in Cornwall, a place I find very inspirational. Trade is very seasonal, hard work in the summer balanced by 3 months holiday in winter when I travel abroad. I have always enjoyed variety, making a wide, continually evolving but always hand-thrown range of designs and colours. My themes at the moment are dolphins, shells and hand-painted clouds. All work is twice-fired in an electric kiln to stoneware temperatures.

Jonathan Garratt

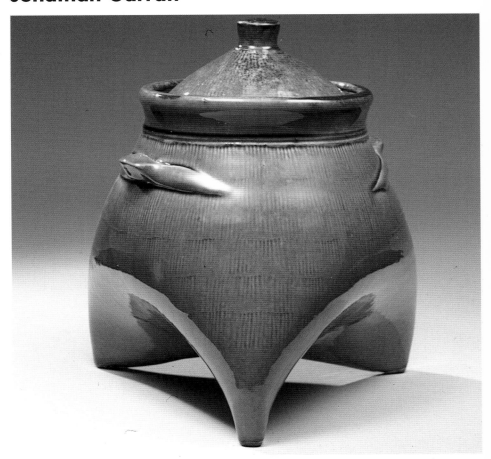

Jonathan Garratt has specialised in making frostproof, wood-fired terracotta pots since 1978. A passion for plants informs many of the designs and firing with wood delivers pots with a wide variety of darker hues than is usual for terracotta. He refines locally dug clay for all the pots and has always made extensive use of roulettes and stamps. African music and textiles and prehistoric pots have considerable influence on his work. He has recently added raw-glazed slipware to the production as well as a small number of "mantlepiece" pots in terracotta. All work wood-fired in 250 cu.ft.round downdraught kiln with 2 tons of wood.

Carolyn Genders Fellow

Carolyn Genders

Carolyn Genders makes individual pieces in high-fired earthenware using vitreous slips, glazes and lustres. She exhibits widely in the UK, Europe and Japan.

Rodney George

Rodney George couldn't stand the competition from all the wonderfully talented potters in England, so he and Esme 'upped sticks, lock stock and barrel' and returned to live in their native and much loved South Africa. He is still very involved in ceramics, with a fine new studio. He is now starting to work with stoneware and porcelain, but not yet doing reduction firing. If all goes well, this is the next big step! Members of the CPA visiting South Africa - specifically the Cape, are most welcome to come and visit. Sadly he finds the competition here just as daunting! There are many, many wonderfully talented people around and their work is exciting and challenging.

Christine Gittins

Christine Gittins South African born and educated, Christine Gittins settled in Wales in 1994 where she is continuing a fifteen year long career as a studio potter. Her pots are wheelthrown in earthenware, finely turned and burnished to a smooth finish. Forms are based on classical shapes and applied surface decoration is kept to a minimum. She likes to explore the unpredictable results from smoking the unglazed, highly burnished vessels. The likeness between the traditional firing methods of the rural African potter and Christine's approach to the surface treatment of her pots bears testimony to the strong influences of African culture. Similarly the classical shapes of her work relate to her formal training and education based on European values and aesthetics. Her work is represented in several public collections in South Africa, and she now exhibits in galleries throughout Britain.

Richard Godfrey Fellow

Richard Godfrey My current work is a mixture of both thrown and hand-built forms. I use a white earthenware body with additions of molochite for larger pieces. The work is decorated with a range of coloured slips which are sprayed, brushed, sponged and trailed over wax and paper resists to provide different depths of image. Glaze firing is to 1140°C in oxidation. I often use areas of dry or textured glazes to provide contrast. The inspiration for my forms and decoration comes from the beautiful countryside and coastline around my studio, particularly things which I find on the beach.

Nigel Graham

Nigel Graham works with wife Christine, in white earthenware. Pieces are thrown and then slip decorated, when bone dry they are raw-glazed with transparent low-solubility glaze, and fired to 1120°C-1130°C. Started potting in1973 and has been full-time potting for sixteen years. Moved to present workshop in 1996. Has exhibited widely and exports to many countries, with standard ranges produced. However more individual pieces are constantly being developed and produced.

Christopher Green Fellow

Christopher Green makes plates and bowls from porcelain which he specially formulates for firing to 1300°C in a reduction atmosphere. Bisque ware is dipped in a base layer of glaze and bisque fired. Then with the aid of wax and latex resist further areas are covered with poured glaze. Finally more glaze and pigments are painted on the ware before firing. Born and educated in Zimbabwe. Trained in Durban, South Africa in the early 70s and then at Goldsmiths' College in the early 80s. Developed software to formulate glazes. Maintains a website for *Ceramic Review* on the Internet.

Paul Green

Paul Green established his present workshop, Abbey Pottery in Cerne Abbas, Dorset in 1986. He is largely self-taught, but completed a workshop training course at Chester School of Art after following a career in historic building conservation. He set up his first workshop in Wensleydale in the Yorkshire Dales, which he ran for six years. Abbey Pottery is a small country workshop producing a wide range of oven and tableware together with some more decorative porcelain. Most of the work is wheel-thrown and fired in a propane gas kiln to 1280°C in a reducing atmosphere. Glazes used are mainly ash, tenmoku, celadon and cobalt blue. The village of Cerne Abbas lies in beautiful countryside 8 miles north of Dorchester, the county town of Dorset. There is a well-stocked showroom at the pottery which is open throughout the year and is situated close to the famous Cerne Giant, a chalk figure carved into the nearby hillside.

Ian Gregory Fellow

Ian Gregory Workshop opened in 1968 producing saltglazed ceramic sculpture. Elected to CPA in 1977 and served on the council for two years. Commissioned by his publisher to write *Kiln Building* in 1977 followed by two other titles *Sculptural Ceramics* and *Kilns*. Work is shown in many galleries world wide, and has examples of his work in many public and private collections including the Victoria and Albert Museum. Guest teaching at many art schools including Harrow, West of England University. Currently producing one-off sculptural pieces, some of which are life-sized figurative work in saltglaze and raku.

Mark Griffiths Fellow

Mark Griffiths Born 1956. We moved to our present workshop, an old school in rural Shropshire in 1983. After ten years of making terracotta garden pots I have returned to high fired stoneware and saltgalzing. All my work is thrown, often repeating familiar shapes. Large pots still hold a particular interest to me and are made regularly. I usually have long making periods of up to four months followed by concentrated sessions of glazing and firing in order to test and develop glazes and decorating techniques. Locally found materials have become the base for all my glazes and new variations are constantly being tried. The showroom at the pottery always has a good selection of work and visitors are very welcome.

Dimitra Grivellis

Dimitra Grivellis designs and makes a collection of finely thrown porcelain bowls, vases, plates, jars and jardinieres. She combines traditional skills with new techniques to create highly individual work. Her love of nature and concern for our diminishing wildlife is the dominant theme of the decoration. Dimitra aims to show wildlife in its natural habitat, sometimes camouflaged or surrounded by culturally relevant patterns. The sharp images are achieved by using sandblasting techniques developed over a number of years to cut the fired clay and glaze. Commissions include murals, mirrors, commemorative plaques, plates and awards for private clients and interior decorators, as well as charity, local government and business sector clients

Barry Guppy

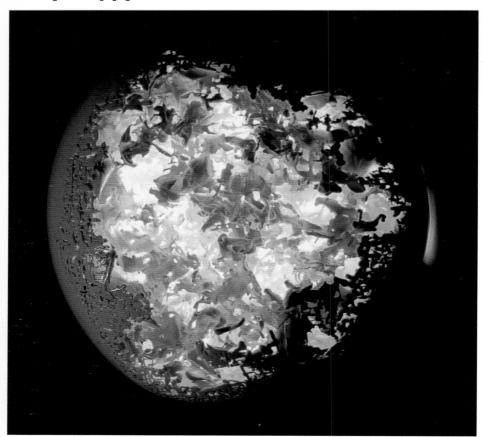

Barry Guppy born in Jersey, Channel Islands in 1937. He is an artist with 26 years experience as a working potter. He was trained and influenced particularly by Hans Coper and Dame Lucie Rie, and taught with them at Camberwell School of Art for many years. Barry has exhibited extensively in this country and abroad. He established his London studio in 1968. At present he is developing fluid structures - natural forms that excite a sense of wonder.

Morgen Hall Fellow

Morgen Hall makes a wide range of domestic tableware, which is often inspired by the food it is intended for, from porridge bowls and tea cabaret sets to large pasta storage jars. Most of the work is wheel-thrown with the emphasis on turning and finishing. Although the work is highly decorated, it is intended for everyday use. (Photography - Patricia Aithie)

Janet Halligan

Janet Halligan Since graduating from Stourbridge College of Art in 1970 I have combined teaching with the development of my own work, and running my workshop. I make 'trompe l'oeil' sculptural work - that is everyday objects like bags, shoes, coats and food, handbuilt in stoneware and glazed and lustred to look very realistic. In the last few years I have also expanded my work into a range of hand-built domestic wares, and more abstract sculptural vessels. As with the trompe l'oeil work , the empahsis is on clarity of form, enhanced by suitable glazes. Influences on this work include architecture, machine forms and surface qualities derived from man-made and natural objects.

Frank Hamer Fellow

Frank Hamer press-moulds plates and dishes which are decorated, often on the back as well, with graphic images taken from nature. The ware is reduced stoneware and all pieces have integral hangers for wall display or can be used as servers. Frank Hamer lives in rural Wales working in a studio which overlooks the Brecon Canal and where studio and kiln space are shared with Janet Hamer. He is co-author of *Clays* and *The Potter's Dictionary of Materials and Techniques*.

Mo Hamid

Mo Hamid I make a range of zircon glazed, hand-thrown stoneware pottery, brush decorated in a variety of colours in the tin glazed earthenware tradition. My work is influenced by Islamic Art, Continental Majolica and Dutch Delftware. Born in London 1960, BA Hons in ceramics 1980-83, West Surrey College of Art and Design. Trained with Alan Caiger-Smith and Edgar Campden at the Aldermaston Pottery1983-86, producing brush decorated tin glazed earthenware. 1986-89 assisted Jonathan Chiswell-Jones, East Sussex, producing brush decorated zircon glazed stoneware. 1989 received Crafts Council setting up grant to establish own workshop in Lewes.

Jane Hamlyn Fellow

JH

Jane Hamlyn Raw-fired saltglaze pots for use and ornament. Work in public collections: Victoria and Albert Museum, and Crafts Council, London, Nottingham Castle Museum, Hanley Museum, Stoke on Trent. Warttembergisches Landsmuseum, Stuttgart, etc.

Caroline Harvie

Caroline Harvie was born in East Kilbride, Glasgow in 1960. She studied ceramics and printmaking at Grays School of Art, Aberdeen (1978-82). After graduating she worked as a graphic artist and then lectured, first at Aberdeen College of Commerce, and then part-time in the ceramics department at Grays. She set up her own ceramics studio in 1990. Her pots are slipcast in bone china and decorated raw with black slip using a combination of paper and latex resist and sgraffito, usually finished with a touch of platinum lustre. Her range includes a variety of vase forms, goblets and candlesticks.

Michael and Barbara Hawkins Fellows

Michael and Barbara Hawkins live and work in the picturesque fishing village of Port Isaac in North Cornwall, where Michael grew up. Their workshop and showroom is in a converted Methodist Chapel and home is in the Sunday School overlooking the harbour. Since moving back to Cornwall the pottery has become more influenced by the themes of the sea and fishing. The pottery is stoneware, with extensive use of lustres and precious metals, and is fired in a 50cu.ft. oil-fired kiln. Their work is sold throughout the country.

Peter Hayes Fellow

Peter Hayes After travelling and working in Africa, India, Japan, and Korea for almost 10 years, Peter Hayes arrived back in England in 1982 and converted a toll house on the banks of the River Avon in Bath. He has developed his thoughts and ideas using many of the techniques and methods learnt on his travels.

Alan Heaps Fellow

ah

Alan Heaps In the early 1960s studied Graphics at the Liverpool College of Art and has been making ceramics full-time for more than twenty years, most of this time in rural Mid-Wales. Each piece is handbuilt by bringing together structures which have been formed in different ways, ranging from slab-work to the use of press moulds derived from natural and manufactured objects. The matt glaze is often used with the addition of stains and matures at 1140° C in an oxidising atmosphere. He has exhibited extensively in Britain and on the continent of Europe, particularly in Germany where he has also held many ceramic workshops.

André Hess Fellow

André Hess makes objects out of clay that recall much more than pottery. He positions his work quite firmly in the wider world of art, design, architecture, and found material, yet manages to refer constantly to the very rich history of ceramics. His objects are always familiar and elusive at the same time. Andre uses any technique that fulfils the requirement. The idea and content are of primary importance. Heavily grogged clay is used for press-moulding, slabwork, and coiling. Surfaces are achieved with slips, oxides, and frit only.

Karin Hessenberg Fellow

Karin Hessenberg I graduated from Camberwell School of Arts and Crafts in 1974. I originally made thrown, burnished and sawdust fired porcelain. My current work is a range of planters, stools, birdbaths and sundials for the garden which were inspired by visits to India and Nepal. My work is handbuilt in Craft Crank stoneware clay. The work is raw glazed and fired to 1260° C in oxidation. Glazes include a matt blue, a green slip glaze and a textured white over reactive slips. I have exhibited widely in Britain and abroad, and I am on the Crafts Council Index. A number of museums have bought my work for their collections, including Glasgow and Stoke on Trent. My plant towers are featured in Malcolm Hillier's book *Container Gardening*. Commissions include a pair of tree containers for the Ferens Art Gallery in Hull. I am the author of *Sawdust Firing*, published 1994, by B.T. Batsford Ltd.

Elaine Hewitt

Elaine Hewitt initially studied three dimensional design and ceramics at Guildford School of Art (1967-71). She spent six years as a repetition thrower in a large pottery before setting up her workshop in Frensham. In 1992 she gained a BA (Hons) in Ceramics at West Surrey College of Art and Design, Farnham and has spent the last five years teaching ceramics part-time at Bedales School, Petersfield. Her work is wheel-thrown using Limoges porcelain, water-etched with many layers of coloured terra-sigillata and finally saggar fired in a gas kiln. Metals, salts and organic materials added to the sawdust give excitingly unpredictable flashes of colour. Her fascination with ancient, once-buried or entombed vessels is reflected in her work with the resulting decorative effects which suggest age and deterioration. Her work is exhibited and sold in the UK and abroad.

John Higgins Fellow

JH

John Higgins The pots that John makes refer most often to architecture, archaeology, and everyday objects. Slab and thrown elements are used in constructions that evolve as they are made. A format is decided, but room is always allowed for spontaneous and expressive handling of the medium. The clay is heavily grogged to withstand the unusual methods of making and the surfaces are treated simply with slips, stains, and oxides. Both gas and electric kilns are used. John always makes pots, but the results continually question and criticise our perception of pottery.

Andrew Hill

Andrew Hill was born in 1964 in Beaconsfield, Buckinghamshire. After completing his Diploma in Ceramics at Derby Lonsdale in 1985, he began working as a potter in his own studio and workshop in Trawden, Lancashire. The influence of eastern ceramics led him to specialise in thrown work as well as the techniques of raku firing. He works with a variety of materials during the reduction including bracken, ferns and sawdust. The result is a dramatic contrast of vibrant, spontaneous colour against a blackened, carbonised body. His work is widely collected and exhibited throughout the UK and Europe.

S. J. Holliday

S. J. Holliday trained as a painter before becoming a ceramist. She works in the lower temperature bands up to 1200°C, firing down the scale, as many as five times, enabling her to achieve the bright colours without burn out. She has exhibited at: the Museum Zeitgenoissche Keramische, Germany; the Royal West of England Academy, Bristol; Blackheath Gallery; the Royal Society of British Artists; Christie's Contemporary Art; the Discerning Eye Exhibition; Look and Like Co., Switzerland; the Usiskin Gallery; the Royal Society of Women Artists; Nan Hai Trust, Australia; and Kaufmann Collection Switzerland. Other work can be found in Israel, Cyprus, Malta, and Germany.

Terri Holman

TH.

Terri Holman After taking a degree at South Glamorgan Institute in 1981, I set up my first workshop in Exeter, then moved to Torquay and then finally to Bovey Tracey in 1994. My work developed in two directions over this period. The porcelain pots are small lidded boxes, bowls and vases, all thrown on the kick wheel and precisely decorated with glazes, enamels and lustres. My stoneware pots on the other hand are much larger and the glazes and enamels are more freely used. My main inspiration is the landscape, especially now that I am living on the edge of Dartmoor.

Ashley Howard Fellow

Ashley Howard Born Maidstone 1963. Studied at Kent Institute of Art and Design, Rochester, between 1983 and 1987. Now working from Herne Bay High School (G.M), Kent, he combines teaching with the production of a range of thrown and altered stoneware. Layers of slip are applied to provide texture before combinations of matt and gloss glazes are added. Together with exhibiting in the UK and abroad Ashley has work in public and private collections. He gives lectures and demonstrations. Between 1993 and 1996 he served on the Members, Associates Advisory Committee of the CPA and is currently a member of the CPA Council.

Joanna Howells Fellow

Joanna Howells Born in 1960 Joanna's first career was in medicine - she took a B.A. in Medical Sciences at Cambridge University. However, in 1984 she decided to pursue, full-time, her love of ceramics. She went to the studio pottery course at Harrow College, from where she graduated with distinction. She works in porcelain, which is wheel thrown and gently altered. A variety of texturing techniques are also used. A range of simple glazes are fired to 1280°C. She exhibits widely in the UK and exports to Europe and the USA.

Anita Hoy Honorary Fellow

Anita Hoy Mainly individual pieces, earthenware, stoneware, porcelain and some raku. Working alone. Trained at Copenhagen College of Art. Started and became head of studio departments at Bullers Ltd. Stoke-on-Trent, and Royal Doulton at Lambeth, working with porcelain and saltglazed stoneware. Looking for oneness of form and decoration, comprising carving, coloured slips and oxide brushwork, under or over clear and opaque coloured reduction fired glazes at 1260°C. Work illustrated in books and articles (*Doulton Lambeth Wares* by D Eyles 1976 and *Studio Porcelain* by Peter Lane 1980). Retrospective Bullers exhibition at Gladstone Pottery Museum 1978 and Doulton Story at Victoria and Albert Museum 1979, Represented with a collection at Victoria and Albert Museum and City Museum, Stoke-on-Trent. Taught for many years at West Surrey College of Art and Design. Work shown at the Crafts Council exhibition 'Influencial Europeans in British Crafts and Design' 1992.

John Huggins Fellow

John Huggins and his assistants make a wide range of frost-proof terracotta plant pots. Most are thrown, some are handpressed. Many of his pots are decorated with a motif of the life-giving forces - the sun and the rain. He also produces large green glazed press-moulded stoneware pots.

Edward Hughes

Edward Hughes having trained at Cardiff and Corsham, a Japanese Government scholarship enabled me to continue my ceramic studies 1977-79 in Kyoto. My first kiln was built by Lake Biwa where I first established my pottery career, having solo exhibitions yearly in Kyoto, Osaka and Tokyo. After seven years in Japan I returned in 1984 to establish my pottery career in England, first at Renwick then at Isel, Cumbria. My work is mostly slip decorated, reflecting my love of 17th century English slipware, high fired in a gas kiln using locally derived ash glazes, reflecting the oriental influence.

Simon Hulbert

Simon Hulbert Following an MA at Cardiff, Simon's first six years were at a studio in South Wales. He has recently settled in Hay on Wye and having completed the renovation of a workshop and gallery, is now developing a new range of work. The larger pieces, usually made to commission, reflect a long standing interest in classical form and proportion. Whilst this is an underlying theme, Simon takes pleasure in adopting a looser approach which exploits the softer qualities of clay. The pots are constructed using a combination of throwing, press-moulding and coiling. They are then high fired to bring out the rich colours of the clay and slips and ensure that they are frost-proof.

Bernard Irwin

IRWIN

Bernard Irwin I trained in painting and sculpture, which has been of major importance in my approach to ceramics. I gained a BA Hons (1st) at Gloucestershire College of Art and Design, then went on a complete post-graduate course at the Jan Van Eyck Academie, in Holland. A regular exhibitor of paintings and sculpture since then, I began making and exhibiting ceramics full-time in 1991. Usually vessels and sculptures, the work is oxidised stoneware handbuilt from slabs. Fusing painting and sculpture they are coloured and textured with sgraffito, engobes and oxides.

Paul Jackson

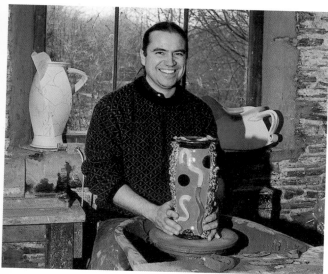

Paul Jackson Thrown vessels are altered to form sculpural pieces, which demand varying decoration, both in colour as well as black and white. From the smallest to the 'floor pieces' the emphasis is on a search for inner strength, energy, excitement and humour.

Anne James Fellow

Anne James The work is made in porcelain, mainly thrown. Some forms are modified by beating. The pieces are covered with coloured slips and burnished while still slightly damp. After biscuit firing they are decorated with layers of resin lustres, using printing, painting and resist techniques. The lustre firing is about 800°C and the pots are taken hot from kiln and smoked in fine sawdust. Ideas are drawn from many sources including the rich colours and surfaces of ethnic textiles. Work can be seen at Fenny Lodge Gallery, Montpelier Gallery, Contemporary Ceramics, and other galleries in UK and Gloucestershire Guild of Craftsmen exhibitions.

John Jelfs Fellow

J.J.

John Jelfs I trained at Cheltenham College of Art and set up present studio in the Cotswolds in 1973. I produce a range of domestic and one-off pieces in stoneware, reduction fired in a gas kiln. For the last ten years I have been concentrating on ash glazes, and am very excited by the simple subtlety achieved on my minimally decorated pots. I sell my work through many galleries as well as directly from my own showroom, and exhibit regularly at home and abroad. I am a current council member of the CPA.

Chris Jenkins Fellow

Chris Jenkins Born 1933. Trained as a sculptor and painter at Harrogate and the Slade School, and as a potter at The Central School, London. In Marsden I produce a range of individual pieces in oxidised stoneware with a continuing theme of asymmetric geometry, using engraved, resisted or masked slips. In France I make woodfired domestic ware.

Wendy Johnson Fellow

Wendy Johnson I studied at Derbyshire College of Higher Education (1988-90). All my work is handbuilt using, slab, pinch and modelling techniques. Inspiration is drawn from many sources including architecture, wildlife and floral images. Each piece of work is individually crafted using white earthenware clay and coloured with body stains and oxides. Work is then biscuit fired to prepare the surface for a final application of oxides and glazes. Colour is also inspired by nature, with deep blues, powdery greens, yellows and subtle pinks. My range includes clocks, candlesticks, vases, lidded boxes and various sized bowls and vessels.

Hazel Johnston Fellow

Hazel Johnston works in porcelain making thrown bottles and bowls. Clarity of form is very important and this together with subtly coloured and textured glaze surfaces are characteristic of her work. A dolomite glaze is used over various mixtures of metal oxides and a restrained use of gold lustre adds emphasis to some forms. All are fired in an 8 cu.ft. electric kiln. Trained at Manchester, N.D.D. 1st class Hons. A.T.D. Taught at Mid-Warwickshire College and produced her own work, slipware, followed by domestic stoneware, then porcelain in the last 14 years. The present studio was set up in 1977.

Philip Jolley

Philip Jolley All my work is handbuilt, by press-moulding, slab building, slipcasting or a combination of these techniques. I use Crank, T-material and porcelain clays as I enjoy the qualities of each. They enable me to portray my fascination for the shape, colour and texture of landscape. Smooth and textured areas; vivid and sombre colours; all combined to create striking forms and mosaic-like decoration. My most recent work is linked to the idea of many sided and viewing points.

David Jones Fellow

David Jones My work is fired using the raku firing process and references both the utensils of the Japanese 'Tea ceremony' and the wares used in the English taking of afternoon tea. The work has also become a vehicle for lustre glaze investigation. In its treatment of form and surface it seeks to interpret both the 'peasant' and 'court' traditions of pottery.

Eileen Jones

Eileen Jones began making pots during her training as an Art and Craft teacher at Goldsmiths' College in the post-war years. She moved from Buckinghamshire to North Devon in 1992 and opened Chapelgate Pottery. She makes a range of stoneware pots in very individual glazes and one-off pieces in porcelain. All the work is fired in an electric kiln.

Walter Keeler Fellow

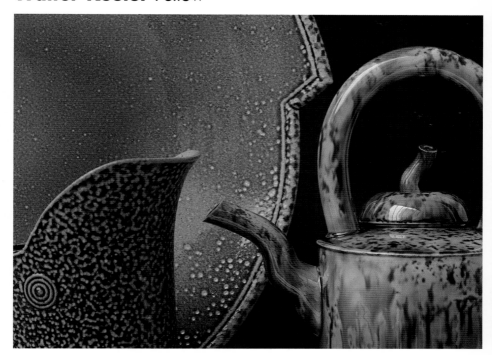

Walter Keeler Trained at Harrow School of Art before the Studio Pottery Course was established. First studio 1965, present studio since 1976. Maker of functional pottery of an individual nature in saltglazed stoneware, some in earthenware.

Julian King-Salter Fellow

Julian King-Salter Born 1954. Full-time potter since 1983. Self taught. Makes individual handbuilt stoneware pots using flattenened coils followed by pinching. Glazes and the combinations in which they are used, are arrived at by intuitive (but carefully recorded) experiment. The method of both making and glazing is essentially spontaneous within an evolving vocabulary, which derives primarily from a direct experience of working with clay, rather than any specific external source. Regular group and solo exhibitions since 1986, recent exhibitions include: Harlequin, Greenwich; Beaux Arts, Bath; and New Millennium, St. Ives. Work is regularly supplied to selected galleries around the country. (Photography Gus Filgate).

Gabriele Koch Fellow

Gabriele Koch Degree in English, History, Political Science at Heidelberg University. Studies and travels in Spain inspired me to want to work with clay. 1979-81 Goldsmiths' College Diploma in Art & Design, Ceramics. 1982 Crafts Council Setting-up Grant. On the Crafts Council Index of Selected Makers. My work concentrates on vessel forms, all pieces are handbuilt, burnished and subsequently smoke-fired. I am interested in the organic development of form and the elemental qualities of the ceramic process. My work has been exhibited widely in the UK and abroad and is housed in many private and public collections including the Victoria and Albert Museum, the Sainsbury Collection, museums in Frankfurt, Karlsruhe, Lorrach and Zurich, art galleries in Aberdeen, Leeds, Gateshead, Aberystwyth Arts Centre and the European Investment Bank in Luxembourg. A monograph has been published by Marston House Books.

151

Anna Lambert Fellow

AYL
Anna Lambert.

Anna Lambert After graduating from Bath Academy of Art in 1980, I set up a workshop, first in Gloucestershire and since 1989 in Yorkshire. My work is all handbuilt earthenware. Methods of coiling, pinching and relief modelling are used to slowly build a variety of domestic forms - candlesticks, egg cups, jugs and large celebratory plates. These are painted with underglaze and lead glazes and reflect in colour and form land and seascape, the weather and seasons. I aim to combine function with evocative and observed images of country life to produce joyful individual pieces. I sell and exhibit my work throughout Britain and in Europe and USA, or by commission.

Peter Lane Fellow

Peter Lane signature

Peter Lane is the author of *Studio Porcelain* (Pitman 1980), *Studio Ceramics* (Collins 1983), *Ceramic Form: Design and Decoration* (Collins 1988), *Contemporary Porcelain: Materials, Techniques and Expressions* (A&C Black 1995) and various articles on ceramics. He has exhibited widely and given numerous lectures and demonstrations in Europe, Australia, New Zealand, Canada and the USA. Most of his work is in porcelain (especially translucent bowls springing from narrow bases) carved, incised, inlaid, or painted with brightly coloured ceramic stains and glazes. Awarded the Silver Medal of the Society of Designer-Craftsmen in 1981. Represented in many public and private collections including the City Museum and Art Gallery, Stoke-on-Trent; City of Aberdeen Museum and Art Gallery; The Castle Museum, Norwich; The Royal Scottish Museum, Edinburgh; The National Gallery of Victoria, Melbourne, Australia; Utah Museum of Fine Arts, Salt Lake City, USA; etc.

David Leach Honorary Fellow

David Leach started in 1930 with father Bernard Leach, as a student, manager and partner at the Leach Pottery, St. Ives until 1956. Now after 67 years potting works alone on thrown stoneware and porcelain, mostly commissions, exhibitions and individual pots. Prices range from £5 to £500. Exhibits regularly in the United Kingdom, USA, Japan and the Continent in group or solo shows. Work in many national and continental museums. Past chairman of the Craft Potters Association and council member of the Crafts Council. Late external assessor for studio pottery courses Harrow School of Art, Scottish Education Department and other colleges of art. Initiated Dartington Pottery Training Workshop 1975 with the late David Canter. Gold Medallist Istanbul 1967. One time Head of Ceramics Department Loughborough College of Art 1953-54. Spends part of each year giving lectures, demonstrations, workshops chiefly in USA, Canada and on the Continent.

Janet Leach Honorary Fellow

Janet Leach was born in Texas, USA in 1918. Moved to New York to study sculpture. Began studying pottery in 1948. Met Bernard Leach, Shoji Hamada and Soetsu Yanagi when they toured America in 1952. Went to Japan to study under Hamada in 1954. In 1956 came to England to marry Bernard Leach and now runs the Leach Pottery in St. Ives, Cornwall making her own individual pots. Likes using several different clays and firing techniques - all reduction stoneware. Has held regular solo exhibitions in England and Japan and her work is included in many national and international shows and collections.

John Leach Fellow

MUCHELNEY

John Leach set up Muchelney Pottery, Somerset with his wife Lizzie in 1964, following an apprenticeship with his father David and grandfather, Bernard Leach. He also trained with Ray Finch and Colin Pearson. He quickly established a reputation for his range of generously rounded hand thrown kitchen stoneware with its unglazed 'toasted' wood-fired finish. It was not until 1983 that he felt able to free himself from the disciplined work ethic of repeat ware to create signed individual pots. These explore a wider range of shapes and creative impulses, and are inspired, in part, by workshop and travel experiences in Europe, America and Nigeria. His pots are in the collections of the Victoria and Albert Museum, the Fitzwilliam Museum, the Crafts Council, the National Museum of Wales and Belfast Museum. Since 1972 John's assistant, master potter Nick Rees has played a key role in standard ware production and the day to day running of the pottery. Student potter Paul Dennis also shares the hard work and excitement of firing the Japanese style climbing kiln..

156

Eileen Lewenstein Honorary Fellow

Eileen Lewenstein makes individual pots and objects in stoneware and porcelain. The sea and its ability to both wear away through constant motion and yet also built up through barnacles and mussels provides a constant fascination and is her main source of inspiration. Recent work has included paired forms; thrown and altered porcelain and coiled stoneware. Exhibited widely in this country and abroad including Greece 1995; Istanbul 1992; Portugal 1990; Australia 1988. Represented in many public and private collections including Victoria and Albert Museum; Glasgow Art Gallery and Museum; Museum of Decorative Arts, Prague; Museum of Contemporary Ceramics, Bechyne, Czechoslovakia; Villeroy and Boch Sculpture Park, Mettlach, Germany; Auckland Institute and Hawkes Bay Art Gallery and Museum, New Zealand. Co-editor *Ceramic Review* Co-editor with Emmanuel Cooper *New Ceramics* Studio Vista 1974.

157

Roger Lewis

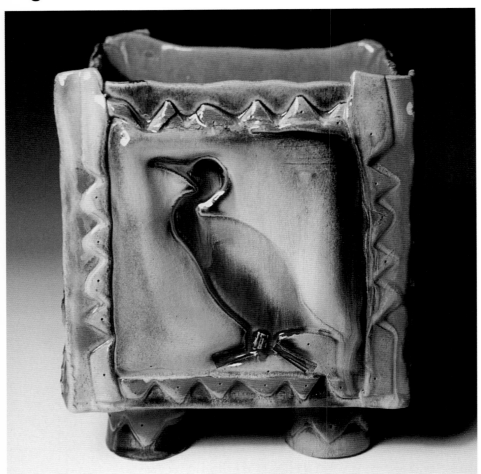

Roger Lewis I trained at Cardiff, in a department that encouraged experiment and individuality. After spending over 20 years as a full-time lecturer and part-time maker, I am starting a new life concentrating on ceramics full-time. My work stems from constant experiment and invention with handbuilding techniques. A period of discovery is followed by a period of subsequent development of image and modification of form. This cycle will now be able to follow a more unforced and natural rhythm uninterrupted by four days teaching a week. Much of my work over the last five years has been decorated by air-brushing underglaze to produce highly coloured surfaces. I have more recently felt the urge to complement this range of work with sculptural stoneware forms produced using similar techniques but without colour.

Gaynor Lindsell

Gaynor Lindsell Her work explores flow, movement and gesture in the form, and seeks to integrate surface, colour and texture. The pots are thrown, ribbed and altered. Working in low fired clays she uses terra sigillata to produce a subtle surface sheen which is enhanced by burnishing. Currently she is exploring the effects of smoked, oxidised, reduction, reoxidised and low salt firings. She trained in sculpture, and later studied and taught ceramics in New York. She set up her own studio in 1988 and worked as assistant to Colin Pearson. She enjoys giving workshops and exhibits in the UK, Europe and USA. Vice-Chair and Council Member of the CPA and Exhibitions Officer.

Andy Lloyd

Andrew Lloyd
Bridport
England

Andy Lloyd Andy Lloyd's designs for contemporary tableware and sculptural vases have been exhibited in London, New York, Los Angeles, Sydney, Melbourne and Amsterdam. In 1993 he set up his present studio in Dorset. Having originally begun with wood-fired ceramics he changed in the 1980s to the technique he is now known for vibrantly colourful hand-painted ceramics. The change grew out of admiration for Mediterranean pottery and an interest in painting. His work brings an expressive delight into the home and the largest most abstract pieces transcend the divide between function and fine art.

Sophie MacCarthy

Sophie MacCarthy My work is thrown, turned then painted with coloured slips, biscuit fired and then glazed with a transparent glaze, fired to 1100°C. I paint the slips directly on to the dry clay surface using large floppy brushes. The slips are absorbed straight away and this immediacy allows for spontaneity and liveliness in the design. It also makes possible mulit-layering of colours which, when combined with wax-resist and stencilling, produces greater tonal depth and bold and distinctive images. My sources of inspiration are varied and wide-ranging; they include landscape, the patterns and movement within it; leaves; water; sky and sea; the human figure.

Christine McCole

LLANBOIDY

Christine McCole Trained at Harrow on the studio pottery course 1977-79. Moved to Wales with her partner, Roger Brann, and converted the smithy in Llanboidy to set up the workshop in 1980. They produce a wide range of domestic stoneware, raw glazed in buff, green and tenmoku, a small quantity of garden stoneware. The pots are wood-fired over 11 hours to 1280°C, in a 40cu.ft. fast fire kiln based on Doug Phillip's version of Fred Olsen's design. Member of the Makers Guild in Wales. The pots are sold mainly from the workshop.

Laurence McGowan Fellow

Laurence McGowan Born Salisbury 1942. Set up own workshop in 1979 after earlier career making maps and interpreting aerial photos in various parts of the world. Trained at Alvingham and with Alan Caiger-Smith, Aldermaston. Traditional majolica decorative techniques employed on quiet, wheel-thrown functional forms. Various stain and oxide mixtures painted on zirconium opacified Cornish Stone based glazes. Electric fired to cone 8 (1260°C). Decorative motifs taken from plant and animal forms, applied to both enhance the pot's form and reflect something of the exuberance of nature. Interests relating to work include lettering/calligraphy and the decorative arts of the Islamic world.

Lesley McShea

Lesley McShea I studied at Caulfield Institute of Technology in Melbourne, where I gained a thorough knowledge of glazes. I returned to England in 1984, and completed a BA Hons. in Ceramics at Middlesex University in 1992 and have been working in my studio since then. I use a stoneware body that I combine myself. It is a mixture of craft crank and white stoneware. I mainly throw on my wheel and also use press moulds to incorporate textures in my work. I use white slip to enhance both the textures and the glaze colour. I mainly use dry, brightly coloured glazes with a high barium content. I produce candleholders, vessels and wall sconces. My work is sold in various outlets mainly in London, Colchester and Brighton.

Vinitha McWhinnie

V₩

Vinitha McWhinnie Born in Sri Lanka and studied science there, but when visiting Britain decided to train in ceramics. Her present ceramics are handbuilt, vessel forms, burnished with coloured terra sigillata and smoked in sawdust, dung or seaweed. First training was as an apprentice with Charles Vyse in Chelsea till moving to the Midlands where she did a diploma and set up her own pottery after travelling worldwide observing a range of ceramic art. It is however the pottery of the Pueblo Indians and her own Sri Lankan heritage that have focused her present work. She exhibits widely including CPA, Bonhams and the Birmingham Museum and Art Gallery. She has recently set up an additional studio in the Custard Factory in Birmingham.

Martin McWilliam

Martin McWilliam   I make saltglaze porcelain domestic ware and coil/slab-built stoneware objects, all wood-fired in a 6 cu/m chamber kiln. 'What I am looking for in my work with clay and fire lies in their own essential beauty and the play between them - a beauty subjective, difficult to define, control or repeat - has something to do with chance coincidence. My methods are as simple/direct as possible where chance has space to suprise. This leads me along a narrow ridge between my will and that of the material.' Born 1957. Bournemouth College of Art 1975-76, Dartington Pottery Workshop 1976-78. Experience in a number of workshops in Europe and Japan 1978-83. In 1983 established own workshop in Germany. Many group and solo exhibitions in Europe and UK. Work in public and private collections. *Ever tried/Ever failed/Never mind try again/Fail Better* (S. Beckett).

166

Jane Maddison

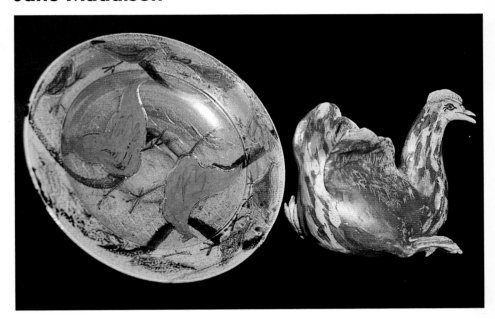

Jane Maddison I studied ceramics at Derby and Croydon and ran my own workshop in West London - 1973-75. I established my current workshop in Lincolnshire in1980. I also work as a part-time lecturer at Melton Mowbray College. I have exhibited widely in Britain and Europe. My main output is highly decorated domestic ware using coloured slips for stoneware. The surface is decorated by a wide range of images. Another facet of my work is *Fabulous Beasts* mounted on columns. Technically I am working with the possibilities of soda firing, this is a new avenue for me which I find both fascinating and exasperating.

Made in Cley

MADE IN
CLEY

Made in Cley is a crafts cooperative established in 1981 comprising six potters and a jeweller: Wolf Altmann, Gunhild Espelage, Richard Kelham, Rosalind Redfern, Robert Wickens, Barbara Widdup and Quay Proctor-Mears (the jeweller). We produce a very wide range of wheel-thrown, reduction and oxidised-fired stoneware for domestic use and also individual sculptural pieces in stoneware, raku and porcelain. We sell our work in our own gallery which is open throughout the year.

Mal Magson Fellow

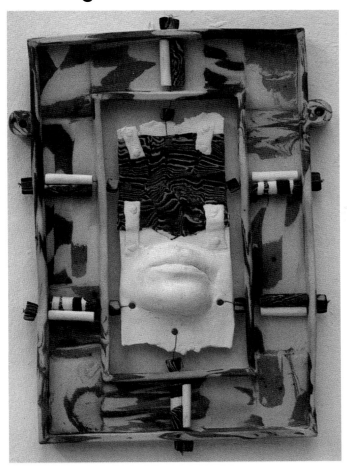

Mal Magson Current work explores the assemblage of cast figurative elements and laminated slabbed structures which integrate stained porcelain and ST material to produce both wall mounted and free-standing forms.

John Maguire

John Maguire Since leaving Duncan of Jordanstone College of Art in 1986, John worked in several locations in Scotland before setting up his present pottery in the basement of the Strathearn Gallery in Crieff. Over the years he has developed and refined his distinctive range of thrown work. In 1995 he received a grant from the Scottish Arts Council to develop extruded forms and was given an artist in residence post at Glasgow School of Art. All the work is made using white stoneware clay, and glaze quality is achieved using cobalt wood ash glazes with over sprays of copper and titanium.

Fenella Mallalieu Fellow

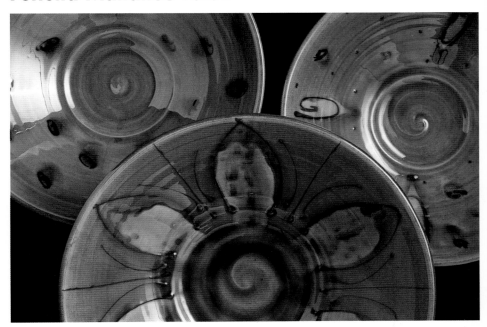

Fenella Mallalieu Thrown lead glazed earthenware for domestic use and visual enjoyment. I have developed seven or eight special high lead glazes which are all food-safe and generally resistant to daily wear.

Jim Malone Fellow

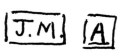

Jim Malone Born 1946. High fired stoneware.

Kate Malone Fellow

Kate Malone London

Kate Malone I make ceramics of varying scale - from egg cups to giant pots weighing a third of a tonne. I make pieces for the kitchen, the collector, architects, interior designers and public spaces....I am inspired by biology and the magic of nature, chemistry and the transformation of clay to ceramic. Techniques include coiling, hand-building, press moulding, hand-modelling and sprigging, earthenware multiple glaze firings and stoneware crystalline glazing. Solo shows in UK, Belgium and the Bahamas. Mixed shows in UK, Japan, USA, Canada, Europe, India. Commissions in hospitals, parks in Exeter, Southampton, Leeds, Bristol, and London. In collections of Manchester City Art Gallery, Bristol, Aberdeen, Hove, Ulster and Stoke-on-Trent museums, Jean Muir, Zandra Rhodes and Andrew Logan.

West Marshall Fellow

West Marshall studied ceramics at Harrow School of Art and set up his first workshop in Norfolk in 1970. He now lives in Buckinghamshire where he has been making small quantities of enamel decorated porcelain domestic ware. Recently he has concentrated on drawing and watercolour painting. He teaches on the Workshop Ceramics (BA Hons) course at the University of Westminster.

Will Levi Marshall Fellow

[signature]

Will Levi Marshall a potter
Fires till cone ten does totter
Reduction fired hues
Gave him the blues
But his oxidised reds are much hotter!
Will Levi Marshall has a B.A. Hons from the Manchester Metropolitan University and an MFA from Alfred University, New York, USA. He currently produces a range of hand thrown functional ceramics spanning tableware to larger individual pieces such as dishes, candelabra and stools. His work is in many museum collections and he lectures throughout the UK. Will Levi Marshall specialises in high temperature coloured glazes fired in an electric kiln.

John Mathieson

John Mathieson started making pottery at evening classes in London, began teaching pottery at secondary level one year later, and has since taken a degree in ceramics. He now pots full-time, making individual pieces and some domestic ware in reduced stoneware, using mainly ash glazes. He has also worked extensively in slipware and raku.

Leo Francis Matthews Fellow

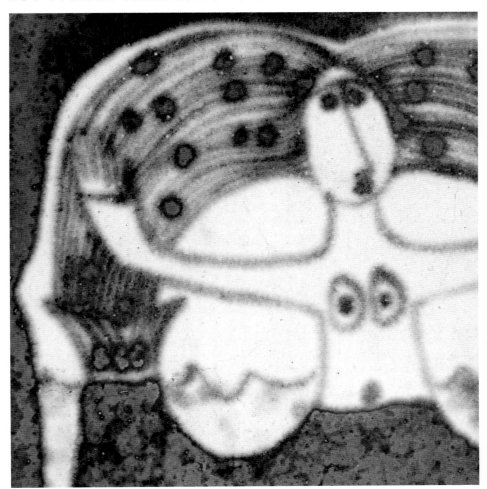

Leo Francis Matthews studied graphics at Manchester College of Art and ceramics at Stoke-on-Trent College of Art. Lectured for twenty-four years at various major colleges of art in Britain. Produced sculptural ceramics, murals and some domestic studio pottery.Explored themes in landscape and trees and aspects of allegory on English decorative arts. Recent journeying through Iran for mosques, tiles and Islamic pottery confirmed the richness achievable from simple indigenous materials at low temperatures. Recent work in small sculptural pieces and tiles with reduced raku using copper pigment with a simple glaze.

Marcio Mattos Fellow

Marcio Mattos Works in red stoneware and 'T' material, reduction fired in a gas kiln. Vessel-orientated individual pieces are entirely handbuilt, with sprayed and brushed glazes emphasising surface texture. Trained initially as a musician and later in ceramics at Goldsmiths' College. Also participated in the International Ceramics Workshop, Tokoname, Japan. Has lectured and exhibited both in Britain and abroad, with work in private and public collections in Britain, Holland, France, Lebanon, Brazil, New Zealand and Japan. As in music, the creative process and spontaneity is important to his work. New studio at the Chocolate Factory, Stoke Newington, London.

Peter Meanley Fellow

pm97

Peter Meanley For the past 10 years I have concentrated almost exclusively on individual saltglazed teapots. Ideas come from seen objects. Increasingly I look at the qualities to be found in different periods of history: Tang; Staffordshire; Islam, to appreciate richness of surface and form. The opportunities presented through a simple spouted pouring vessel are enormous and still excite me. Presently a senior lecturer in the School of Fine and Applied Art in the University of Ulster at Belfast.

Eric James Mellon Fellow

Eric James Mellon

in foot a : 1994 ... Ath used title

Eric James Mellon Born 1925. Studied Watford, Harrow and Central School of Arts & Crafts, London. Creates brush drawn decorated ceramic fired 1300°C, using tree and bush ash glazes. Represented in the Victoria & Albert Museum and collections in Britain and internationally. 'Drawing on to clay is firing thoughts into ceramic. The concern is not academic correctness in drawing but to create work of visual decorative poetic surprise and aesthetic satisfaction'.. See: Rogers P. *Ash Glazes* (Black/Chilton 1991) and 'Magic and Poetry ' *Ceramic Review* No. 114, 1988.

Kate Mellors

Mellors

Kate Mellors I trained at Camberwell School of Art 1972-75 and on leaving shared a workshop in London and taught part-time in adult education. I made a range of tableware and also individual thrown and decorated pieces. In 1980 I set up a workshop at home and started making stoneware garden pottery in 1985. This new direction arose from my interest in gardens, traditional architecture and garden pottery. Travel in the Far East in 1986 provided further inspiration. The larger scale work needed more space and in 1990 I moved to West Dorset to start a new pottery in a converted farm building. I now work full-time making a range of garden lanterns, bird-baths, planters, stools and fountains. These are all once-fired to 1280°C.

Nick Membery

Nick Membery I make reduction fired stoneware. My pots are all thrown, although they are often altered and I incorporate press moulding, extruding, rolling and slab building. I am influenced by the making process and by usable vessels of any nature. While the work I produce is of a traditional nature, I feel the appearence and style is modern and that my pots are well suited for use in both traditional and contemporary kitchens and homes.

Jon Middlemiss Fellow

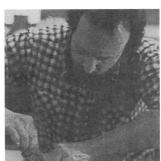

Jon Middlemiss Making sculptural and vessel forms full time since 1979. Exhibitions in UK, Belgium, Germany, Holland, France, Italy and USA, including touring exhibitions, lectures, demonstrations. Awarded Gold Medal 13th Biennale, Vallauris 1992. Honourable Mentions at Mino Triennale, Zagreb Triennale with other awards in Germany and Belgium. Collections include Keramion, Kestner and Cologne Museums. Opening of Keramik-Studio-Middlemiss, Germany 1990. Member of Chambre-Syndicale des Ceramistes et Ateliers, and Crafts Council Index. 'A major influence has been the ceramics of the natives of Arizona which reflect a sense of order based on the foundations of a spiritual philosophy that sees even the harshest of life's experiences as meaningful and of consequence. Meditation offers me the same foundation."

David Miller Fellow

David Miller Born in London. Studied sculpture, printmaking and ceramics at Ravensbourne and Brighton Colleges of Art. Set up workshop in London in the 1970s. Now living and working in Southern France making one-off pieces and a range of highly decorated functional ware based on traditional French slipware. Exhibitions in France, Holland, England and Germany.

Sean Miller

Sean Miller After completing the BTEC HND course at Harrow I set up my own workshop in London in 1991. I make a range of functional thrown and slipped earthenware pottery for domestic use. I use Fremington clay and the slip-trailed decoration is inspired by traditional European slipware on folk pottery.

Toff Milway Fellow

Toff Milway Saltglaze country potter specialising in high temperature stoneware using pure clay slips, adapting some traditional slipware techniques to produce finely textured surfaces on a variety of domestic ware and individual dinner services, all in saltglaze. Large and decorated pieces always available. Extended periods abroad working in Africa and USA. I now live and work in the beautiful Cotswold village of Conderton, and sell all I make from my own studio gallery. Commissions undertaken. Occasional exhibitions. Member of the Gloucestershire Guild of Craftsmen.

Jill Moger

Jill Moger 3/97

Jill Moger Recently elected an Associate of the Society of Wildlife Artists exhibiting annually at the Mall Galleries. Work included in public and private collections in Britain and abroad. Exhibited and auctioned by Bonhams in Singapore. Handbuilt wildlife subjects, predominantly reptiles, in stoneware and porcelain. Intricately detailed with various stains and lustres.

Ursula Mommens Honorary Fellow

Ursula Mommens I studied for two years under William Staite Murray at the Royal College of Art and much later had the great good luck of working with Michael Cardew at Wenford Bridge. I started off converting an old cowhouse in Kent and after marriage to Julian Trevelyan worked at Durham Wharf, Hammersmith Terrace, London. I now work at the pottery I set up 37 years ago in South Heighton, Newhaven, making useful stoneware using mainly wood ash glazes on our own body - fired in Chris Lewis's big wood-fired kiln or my small gas one.

Sarah Monk

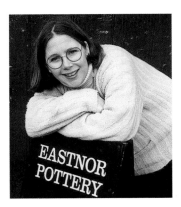

SARAH
MONK
SM

Sarah Monk I graduated from Bath in 1992. Everything I make has a specific use coupled with a sense of fun and playfulness. For example, I produce a range of breakfast ware including toast-racks, egg cups and spoons, decorated with birds and fruit, designed to start the day on a cheery note. I enjoy the warmth and colour of earthenware glazes and for this reason choose to work in white clay. After taking part in an exhibition called 'Bugs' at the Simon Drew Gallery in 1996 my work has since featured caterpillars, buterflies and bees. Pieces are thrown, slab built and modelled. Finally sprigs are applied, with some help from my assistant Juliet Neale. My work is regularly seen in galleries around the UK. I also have a showroom at Eastnor Pottery which I share with fellow potter Jon Williams.

Kim Morgan

Kim Morgan was born in Palmerston North in New Zealand. Having studied and gained experience in New Zealand and Australia, and having travelled abroad extensively, he has now settled with his family, and opened his own workshop and gallery, Morgan Pottery, in Jersey, Channel Islands. This is his only outlet which produces a wide range of domestic stoneware and limited pieces.

Aki Moriuchi Fellow

Aki Moriuchi Born in Tokyo, Japan. Trained in ceramics at Harrow College (Westminster University), and Middlesex University. Works in North London. Producing weathered looking texture-glazed stoneware, incorporating some gestural elements. Most of them are multi-glazed and multi-fired, with the use of sandblast technique. She also make Japanese tablewares.

Jenny Morten

JM

Jenny Morten A former student at York Art School and Central School of Art, Jenny established her first studio in London in 1972. She has exhibited widely in he UK and abroad and her work combines throwing, slabbing and coiling to produce vessels which explore the possibilities of sculptural form through the building process and surface treatment. Using smooth white stoneware bodies enables the surface to evolve with sgraffito, painted oxides, wax and coloured slips. Jenny has recently completed a period as Artist in Residence in two schools in the North East of England and works from her studio in Darlington.

Roger Mulley

Roger Mulley Very large thrown and sculptural vessels using high colour and natural textures inspired by nature. Work is exhibited regularly and sold through the pottery showroom at Clanfield in South Hampshire. Visitors are welcome. Roger Mulley's ceramics can be found in collections in both the UK and abroad.

John Mullin

John
Mullin

John Mullin was born in Lancashire in 1949. He studied at Burnley and Cardiff (where he obtained a First Class Hons. in Ceramics), and Hornsey (ATC). After some years teaching in Further Education he began in 1980 earning his living solely from making ceramics and has done so ever since. John's pots are influenced by classical forms and painted with coloured slips depicting images of animals. Besides having exhibited widely in England, John has also exhibited in Germany, the Netherlands, and Japan. He has work in permanent collections in Germany and Japan. John lives with his family in Devon.

Sue Mundy

Sue Mundy creates one-off stoneware vessels from handbuilding techniques. With form and texture being fundamental in her making she uses slips, oxides and a reduction firing of 1250°C to help her achieve individual tactile pieces.

Stephen Murfitt

SM

Stephen Murfitt Educated at Cambridge School of Art, West Surrey College of Art and Design (Farnham), and the Middlesex Polytechnic (Hornsey College) from 1972-78. Since leaving college I have combined teaching with making ceramics and have recently established my current workshop near Wicken Fen in Cambridgeshire. The pots, which are mainly handbuilt and raku fired, have been exhibited in galleries throughout Britain, and included in many private and public collections. Recent outlets have included: The Hart Gallery, London and Nottingham, The CCA Gallery, Cambridge, The Todd Garner Gallery, Glasgow and Bonhams, London.

Tessa Wolfe Murray

Tessa Wolfe Murray trained at Goldsmiths' College 1982-84. I set up a workshop in London until 1995 when I moved to Yorkshire, sharing a studio and working part-time for Anna Lambert. In 1996 I joined a multi-disciplined studio in Leeds situated in an old mill. Apart from a small slip-cast range, all my pots are slab-built and functional. The surface decoration is coloured slip, sprayed or brushed on, to build up depths of surface with layers. After glaze firing in an electric kiln to 1100°C, the pots are sawdust fired in the open air very quickly, a method I developed to suit ware that is slab-built and glazed internally. I sell my work through craft and fine art galleries in the UK, Europe and Japan.

Emily Myers Fellow

Emily Myers is known predominantly for her vibrant blue stoneware ceramics. She has recently developed a complementary range of terracotta work with an equally striking glaze surface. The range of work includes dishes, vases and jars which are all thrown on the wheel to achieve controlled forms and clean lines. The lidded boxes are inspired by the domes and minarets of Islamic architecture. Emily's work can be seen in London at the Crafts Council Shop and at Contemporary Ceramics, and in New York at the Guggenheim Museum shop.

Susan Nemeth Fellow

Nemeth

Susan Nemeth This collection of porcelain (above) is inspired by the cut-out collages of the painter Matisse. Susan has developed a unique method of decoration. The decoration is an integral part of the work. Each piece is made of many layers of inlaid porcelain stained clays and layers of coloured slips. The work is press-moulded and high fired. Bowls, platters, vases and one-off fine tableware pieces are also available to commission. Susan has exhibited in Europe, Japan and USA. She is on the Crafts Council Selected Index of Makers.

Christine Niblett

Christine Niblett I was born in Cheshire but moved to live in Palma de Mallorca in 1966. Initial studies included four years at the Palma School of Applied Arts (Ceramics). Now working solely in laminated millefiore porcelain, body-stained with natural metal oxides and reduction-fired to 1260°C. The Mediterranean environment can perhaps be seen in the flowing patterns and clear colours integrated into the forms. I enjoy participating in exhibitions, symposia and competitions in Europe whenever possible, which in the past have included Arte-Fiera, Bologna; Ob'Art, Paris; Siklos International Ceramics Symposium and Kecskemet International Ceramic Studio, both Hungary; International Biennial of Ceramic Art, Vallauris (1988, 1990, 1992, 1994).

Jacqueline Norris

JN
eton

Jacqueline Norris My training was at Harrow (1985-87) and the Royal College of Art (1987-89). I work with a range of techniques appropriate to the particular piece I am making. Coiled pots (above) are made with T material. Tile panels, caskets and planters are made with a slab roller using a T material and porcelain mix. Small urns and lidded jars are thrown. Egyptian artefacts are my main source of inspiration; life in the sea is a close second.

Evelyn Papp

Evelyn Papp Born 1936. Trained Derby 1987/9. Individual tin-glazed earthenware ceramics. Present range includes plates bowls jugs and platters. Mainly thrown on an electric wheel. After bisque firing, pots are dipped in tin glaze and decorated - majolica style. Watercolour effects are achieved using oxides, body stains and pigments, building up in layers. Free brushwork, sponging and sgraffito methods employed. The white ground providing an inviting and challenging surface. Graphic imagery derives from numerous sources. Italian medieval ceramics, marine life, floral and geometric motifs. Glaze firing to cone 2, electric kiln. Work sold through galleries, exhibitions and workshop. Certain commissions undertaken. Licentiate of the Society of Designer Craftsmen.

Stephen Parry

Stephen Parry Trained at Croydon College of Art 1974-77, Dartington Pottery Workshop 1977-79, and in France using wood-fired kilns. Set up present pottery in Norfolk in 1981, making a range of domestic ware and one-off pots, using both stoneware and porcelain clays. Glazes are made from different types of wood ash. Pots are fired in a 120 cu.ft. crossdraft wood-fired kiln to 1300°C. He is a part-time tutor at Camberwell College of Arts, teaching throwing and kiln building.

Colin Pearson Honorary Fellow

Colin Pearson Born London 1923. Studied painting at Goldsmiths' College. Makes individual pieces in porcelain and stoneware. Winner of the 33rd Grand Prix at Faenza, Italy, and in 1980 was awarded a major Crafts Council Bursary for study in the Far East. Has work in many public and private collections. Has done regular workshops and slide presentations in the UK, on the Continent, USA, Malaysia and Australia. A member of the International Academy of Ceramics, and on the Crafts Council Slide Index. Honorary Fellow of the London Institute, Honorary Member of London Potters and Honorary Fellow of the CPA.

Katrina Pechal

Katrina Pechal I studied at Camberwell School of Art and opened my studio in 1993. My work is thrown and fired to 1230°C in an electric kiln. Surfaces are made up of layers of slips under a lithium glaze. Silicon carbide in one of my slips causes the glaze to pit and pull away from itself, revealing the layers beneath. I have shown my work in a number of galleries around the country, including with Jack Doherty at Montpellier in Stratford-upon-Avon. I also teach pottery part-time for Wandsworth Adult College, which includes running a five day raku course every summer.

Carol Peevor

Carol Peevor

Carol Peevor I trained at Wolverhampton University from1975-79, setting up a small studio as soon as I left, in Wolverhampton. I produced buttons and small items which I sold at craft fairs. I now live and work in Wednesbury, my studio being in the garden. I use white stoneware or earthenware clay to make my pots, which are all one-off designs. Press-moulding has been my main forming method, although I now use coiling , slabbing and throwing to alter forms. I use oxides and underglaze colours and sometimes glazes. I work by intuition, never really having an end in view - often I will alter forms as I go along. I particularly like bottle forms and creating pictures - usually to do with my life or likes.

Jane Perryman Fellow

Jane Perryman trained at Hornsey College of Art and later spent a year at Keramisch Werkcentrum in Holland. I make coiled vessel forms which are burnished and after bisque firing treated with various resist techniques before smoke firing. Inspiration comes from Indian, African and early Celtic pottery. I exhibit and give workshops in the UK and internationally. My book *Smoke -Fired Pottery* was published in 1995; I am currently researching *Traditional Indian Pottery* to be published in 1999 by the same publisher A&C Black.

Richard Phethean Fellow

Richard Phethean trained at Camberwell, graduating in 1976, and in the studios of Colin Pearson and Janice Tchalenko making domestic stoneware. Drawn to early English slipware, a lengthy exploration of the medium ensued. A personal style evolved, significantly influenced by a two year period working as a crafts project V.S.O. in Papua New Guinea. Latterly my approach to form and decoration has relaxed, revisiting earlier themes to develop a new domestic range. Smaller items are produced in limited editions with larger pieces;- jugs, bowls casseroles, platters, trays and a series of rectangular press moulded dishes. Teaches at Harrow College, and offers studio based one-to-one tuition and monthly weekend courses in throwing. Author of *Throwing* in the *Complete Potter* series and producer of a series of throwing video cassettes.

John Pollex Fellow

John Pollex trained at Harrow College of Art, 1968-70, after which he was assistant to Bryan Newman and Colin Pearson. He set up his own workshop in 1971 and established his reputation producing traditional slip decorated ware. In the mid 1980s he felt the need for a change. He now produces highly individual thrown and altered forms, these are richly painted with coloured slips. The images are usually abstract and often reflect his interest in Eastern meditative philosophies. He particularly enjoys the personal contact to be found in lecture/demonstrations and has featured in over 50 workshops given in the UK and overseas.

Philomena Pretsell

Philomena Pretsell Edinburgh College of Art 1987-89 (BA Hons) Diploma in Post-Graduate Studies 1989-1990. All Pretsell's work is slab-built, slip-decorated earthenware. Building pots with slabs gives tremendous scope to the imagination and the variations are endless.The slab is first decorated with slips and sometimes wooden printing blocks are used to make impressions in the clay. In this way the clay can be treated like a piece of fabric and the pattern and form fall naturally into place when assembled. Of the transfers Pretsell enthuses 'I love using them, they have a wonderful quality of decorativeness and a hint of nostalgia.'

Ursula Morley Price

Ursula Morley Price graduated in painting at Camberwell College of Art and The Slade. Ursula makes one-off handbuilt forms. She fires her work, both in reduction and oxidation to cone 7. Her pots are often glaze fired 5 or 6 times to obtain the colour and texture she requires. During the last three years Ursula's work has developed from bottle forms with mantles to her present slender necked vases. Ursula exhibits widely in Europe and America. Her work is in many private and public collections, among which are: Museum of Modern Art, New York; Los Angeles County Museum; Hamburg Museum; Keramikmuseum Hohr-Grrenzhausen and the Musee des Arts Decoratifs, Paris. Ursula frequently gives slide talks and workshops in the UK, Belgium, France and America. Her work is regularly sold at Bonhams contemporary ceramics sales.

Paul Priest

Paul Priest Originally trained in graphic design and illustration. Learnt ceramics by trial and error. Uses animal and bird forms as a vehicle and is concerned with texture and movement rather than an exact anatomical reproduction of the creature, the stylisation and presence of the piece being of all importance. My work is, after all, totally ornamental, having no functional use, it must therefore evoke something by way of reaction from the observer or I have failed. Influences are drawn from many sources on an ever changing basis. 'May the work speak for itself'.

Nick Rees

MUCHELNEY

Nick Rees trained and worked with John Leach since 1972. He produces much of the catalogue range of pots at Muchelney Pottery and manages the firing of the two-chambered wood-fired kiln. His individual pots are mainly bottle and bowl forms - often altered after throwing by carving, faceting or indenting to accentuate the form. Work is in both porcelain and stoneware and is wood-fired.

Gaynor Reeve

Gaynor Reeve

Gaynor Reeve I have explored most aspects of ceramics since I began in 1982; and by being self-taught gave me the challenge of developing and creating a style that I still enjoy today. My love of abstract art has always influenced my work when producing wall plates, bowls and vases which I decorate with bold, highly coloured lively designs, using coloured slips. The plates and bowls are wheel thrown, using a white earthenware clay. The vases, which are also wheel thrown are given height by adding coils of clay. After biscuit firing, my pots are then clear glazed and fired in an electric kiln to 1130°C. I have recently begun to experiment with slab work, which enables me to explore various techniques and methods of decoration on wall hangings.

Peter Reynolds

Peter Reynolds I initially studied Fine Art at Goldsmiths' School of Art from 1978-81. After two years of post graduate study in Brighton, I went to Japan in 1984, intending to study printmaking. However, I became increasingly drawn to ceramics and began to study pottery, first in Tokyo from 1986 and then in Hagi from 1988-89. I set up Balaclava Pottery in 1992 where I produce lustre-decorated stoneware, specialising in marbling techniques.

Mary Rich Fellow

Mary Rich was born in Cornwall and started her first workshop in Cornwall in 1962, having studied painting and ceramics at Bournemouth College of Art with David Ballantyne. This was followed by workshop experience with Harry and May Davis at the Crowan Pottery in Cornwall, and David Leach in Devon. For 20 years the work was once-fired saltglaze, but since the early 80s the pots have been made in porcelain using a propane kiln with decoration in gold and various lustres. Member of Devon Guild of Craftsmen, past chairman of Cornwall Crafts Association.

Christine-Ann Richards Fellow

CAR

Christine-Ann Richards Trained at Harrow School of Art and Technology (1971-73) under Mick Casson. Worked for Bryan Newman and David Leach. Started own workshop within Barbican Arts Group (1975-83). I now live and work at home. The 1978 CPA trip to China had a radical effect on my work and way of life. Since then I have studied Chinese art, taken people to China and continued developing my own work. I produce thrown porcelain as well as large vitrified earthenware vessels suitable for interiors, conservatories and gardens. Some of these have incorporated water features. Work in public and private collections. Exhibits at home and abroad. I work alone.

Audrey Richardson

Audrey Richardson trained originally in painting and sculpture at Duncan of Jordanstone College of Art, Dundee, Scotland. Started potting through attending local evening classes. Works alone, making individual pots and sculptures. These are handbuilt using mainly T-material, then decorated with a selected range of slips and glazes. The work is fired to 1250°C. Also undertakes large garden sculptures and portraits on commission. Has recently moved house and workshop to scenic Pembrokeshire. Showcase of current work on display.

David Roberts Fellow

David Roberts is known for his coil built, raku fired ceramics. He has exhibited his work throughout the UK and abroad. Work is represented in many public and private collections, including the Victoria and Albert Museum, Royal Museum of Scotland, Ulster Museum and the Museum of Wales. Workshops and demonstrations are regularly held in the UK and Europe.

Hilary Roberts

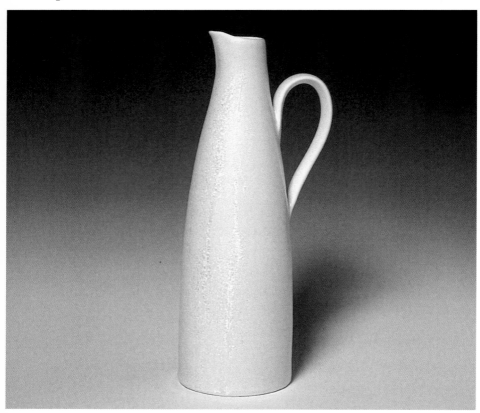

Hilary Roberts I make a range of porcelain tableware and other functional pots. Some of my work is constructed from low-relief decorated slabs, but most is thrown and decorated either with different white glazes or with low-relief stamps.

Jim Robison Fellow

Jim Robison As a practitioner, his studio time is divided between slabware vessels and sculptures and large scale commission pieces. Most recently he has completed relief sculptures for the entrance of the Civic Hall in Holmfirth, and businesses in Wakefield. Other commission sites include the Grafton shopping centre, Cambridge, the Calum Country Park, Dewsbury, and Leicester Royal Infirmary. Also an author, his recently published book *Large Scale Ceramics*, documents the making of these architectural sculptures, as well as including examples from around the world. He also teaches part-time at Leeds University College, Bretton Hall; with the help of his wife Liz promotes ceramics through exhibitions at their own gallery.

Phil Rogers Fellow

Phil Rogers Born in Newport, South Wales in 1951. Came to live and work in Mid Wales in 1977 and moved to our present site half a mile outside Rhayader in 1984. Most of my pots are thrown and then fired in either a 75 cu.ft. downdraught reduction kiln or saltglazed in a 40 cu.ft. catenary kiln, which is about to be replaced after 10 years of salting. I make extensive use of wood ash and local stones, clays etc. for the glazes in both kilns. Our series of summer workshops are continuing to attract potters from all over the world. I have exhibited in many galleries both in the UK and abroad and pots are held in a number of public collections, most notably the National Museum of Wales, Newport Museum and Art Gallery, University of Wales Collection, Aberystwyth, City Museum, Hanley, Stoke on Trent, William Ismay collection, and others. Private collections particularly in USA and Japan. 1993 and 1995 visited Ethiopia to oversee the women's pottery project in Gondar. 1996 gave workshops to township people in Capetown South Africa. Have also made a number of workshop and lecture tours in the USA. Member of the Crafts Council Selected Index of Makers and author of *Ash Glazes* (A&C Black 1991) and *Throwing Pots* (A&C Black 1994). Past Chairman of the Craft Potters Association.

Duncan Ross Fellow

Duncan Ross established his present workshop near Farnham in 1989, after a period of study and exploration into terra-sigillata techniques. He has work in many important public and private collections including the Victoria and Albert Museum. His in-depth knowledge has enabled him to refine the ancient use of terra-sigillata slip creating an exhuberant and sophisticated result. He has developed a unique process using resisted layers of polished slip applied to finely thrown forms; his highly controlled use of smoke firing produces a warm chestnut orange and deep earth browns and blacks. He is on the Crafts Council Index of Selected Makers.

Elizabeth Roussel

Elizabeth Roussel trained at Antioch University (USA) and Goldsmiths' College (London); holder of In Service diploma, London University 1985; member of the Oxfordshire Craft Guild. I concentrate mainly on wheel-thrown stoneware and porcelain bowls, vases and plates, fired to reduction 1285°C. Each pot is a one-off and often made to commission. The pieces are richly decorated with motifs drawn from nature. The work is particularly suitable for commemorative occasions, to celebrate for example weddings and anniversaries, where calligraphy becomes an integral part of the design.

Antonia Salmon Fellow

Antonia Salmon Studied Geography at Sheffield University (1979-81) and then trained in Studio Pottery at Harrow School of Art (1981-83). In 1984 spent one year travelling in the Middle East and Northern India. Since 1985 I have worked on one-off and limited editions of burnished and smoke-fired sculptures and pots. These are all characterized by my interest in exploring the qualities of movement and stillness in form and space. Work is exhibited in Britain, Europe and the USA.

Robert Sanderson

Robert Sanderson I've been involved in wood-firing ever since I left college in 1975. Initially during an apprenticeship, and afterwards while travelling in Tanzania, New Zealand and eventually Australia. Returning to my native Scotland in 1985 together with my wife Coll Minogue, we established our current studio, and built a single chambered Bourry box type kiln from recycled firebricks. My work continues to evolve to take advantage of those qualities and effects achievable by woodfiring over a 24 hour cycle. Grants: The British Council, The British American Arts Association. Awards: 1994 - The Scottish Arts Council Crafts Bursary, 1997 - Winston Churchill Travelling Fellowship.

Patrick Sargent Fellow

Patrick Sargent studied wood-firing and trained at Farnham (W.S.C.A.D.) under Paul Barron and Henry Hammond 1977-80. Established present workshop in the Emmental region of Switzerland in 1994. Wood-fires a five cubic metre anagama with demolition timber to 1320°C. Firings lasting around 80 hours. Pots for use are made using simple momentum wheels and wooden moulds, with several clay bodies mixed by foot. A wide variety of thrown qualities are achieved as a result of intensity and duration of the firing, the style of kiln packing and the desposit of ash. Exhibitions and demonstrations in the UK and Europe.

Nicolette Savage

Nicki
1997

Nicolette Savage N.D.D; A.T.C. I graduated from Goldsmiths' in pottery and printmaking, and I continue to work equally in both disciplines. Urns and water features are amongst my largest pieces, but I am also developing a range of small lidded animal and bird vessels. Drawing and etching influence the decoration of my pots, which are often deeply carved and multi-surfaced. I seldom glaze, prefering the simplicity of oxide washes on a craft crank body, fired to 1260°C. I work mostly to commission and exhibit mainly in Kent and Sussex. I teach both pottery and printmaking for Adult Education in Bromley.

Micki Schloessingk Fellow

Micki Schloessingk wood-fired saltglaze.

David Scott Fellow

D.S.

David Scott Born in Yorkshire, studied Stoke-on-Trent and Royal College of Art. Over recent years the work I have made has varied from the strictly functional at one extreme to periods of time exploring abstract non-functional themes. I am a full-time lecturer running a degree course in ceramics at Loughborough College of Art and Design, and this activity both constrains and stimulates my making, but allows me to pursue areas of the craft as they interest me with a measure of independence. Work in various public and private collections including the Victoria and Albert Museum.

Sheila Seepersaud-Jones

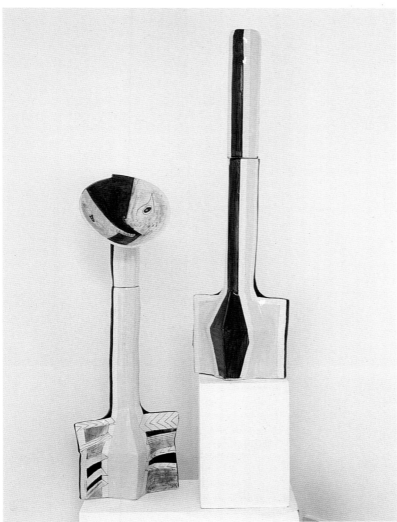

Sheila Seepersaud-Jones Born in Guyana. I taught English before coming to England to train as a nurse. Later I developed my interest in art and achieved a BA Hons in Fine Art, St.Martins School of Art, London. As initially I was concerned with exploration of three dimensional forms I chose to do my degree in sculpture. Latterly I have concentrated on clay to explore texture, colour and pattern on three dimensional surfaces. Work is both sculptural and traditional. I make coiled, slabbed and thrown pots fired at 1100°C - 1250°C. I hand paint my pieces in designs which reflect my Caribbean and European backgrounds.

Sarah-Jane Selwood Fellow

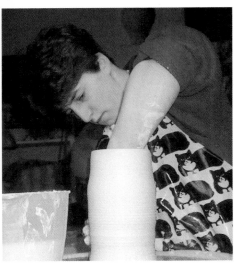

Sarah-Jane Selwood In October 1992 Sarah-Jane Selwood established her studio in Edinburgh. She works predominantly in porcelain, thrown on the wheel then distorted and incised. Reduction fired to 1280°C. Her work is exhibited widely in Britain and abroad. Solo shows include: The Oxford Gallery, The Scottish Gallery, Edinburgh, Contemporary Ceramics, London, The Convention Centre, Hong Kong and Galerie L, Hamburg Germany. Her ceramics were also selected for exhibition in the Bienniale Internationale de Ceramique D'Art, Vallauris (1994), the Fletcher Challenge Ceramics Exhibition, New Zealand 1995, and Talente 1995, Munich, Germany.

Ken and Valerie Shelton

Valerie Shelton.

Ken and Valerie Shelton produce their pottery in partnership at their home in Cheshire. Pots are thrown by Ken, usually bowls up to 18" diameter, in white earthenware. The work is decorated by Valerie in underglaze colours. Ken learned to pot in the 60s, training with potters in Bristol and London. He combines the pottery work with work for a leading kiln manufacturer. Valerie studied fashion design at Brighton and Bristol art colleges. Design commissions include tableware hand decorated in Slovenia and porcelain mugs from Poland. She works full-time in the pottery. Work is sold through retail galleries.

Ray Silverman Fellow

Ray Silverman Trained at Camberwell School of Art and Crafts, London and University of London Goldsmiths' College. Chairman of London Potters, Fellow of the Society of Designer-Craftsmen. On the Crafts Council Index. Solus Exhibitions including Victoria and Albert Museum, London (Man Made Series). Exhibited widely in group exhibitions throughout the world. My work has ranged from thrown tableware, handbuilt pieces to working as a designer and consultant in the ceramic industry. Over the past 20 years I have devoted the time in my workshop to producing individual thrown forms in porcelain and stoneware.

Penny Simpson

Penny Simpson started making pots during a three year stay in Japan. She is the author of *The Japanese Pottery Handbook* (Kodansha 1979). From 1979-81 Penny trained at Dartington Pottery in Devon. Penny uses red earthenware clay, decorated with coloured slips to produce a range of hand thrown pots including bowls, jugs, plates, lamp-bases and plant pots. She also decorates tiles, making panels for kitchens and bathrooms as well as a range of individual tiles.

Graham Skinner

Graham Skinner Born 1966. Studied ceramics at Medway College of Art and Design 1984-88. Set up present studio in Rochester in 1989. Most of my pots are thrown on the wheel. I use a combination of different slips and glazes, fired in a propane kiln in a reduction atmosphere to 1300°C.

Michael Skipwith Fellow

 s

Michael Skipwith Lotus Pottery was founded in 1957 by Michael and Elizabeth Skipwith who had first met as students at Leeds College of Art. From 1957-79 they ran the pottery employing up to 17, making green glazed domestic earthenware fired in electric kilns. In 1980 after converting part of their large old- stone built farm Michael recommenced potting on his own using a wood-fired kiln which gives a rich toasted colour to unglazed pots, particularly suited to garden pots. He also makes glazed kitchenware and more recently porcelain bowls and vases. He is the Devon stockist of Potclays range of clays and raw materials.

Daniel Smith

Daniel Smith On leaving Harrow college in 1994 he helped set up Archway Ceramics in Bow, East London. He produces a range of hand thrown domestic porcelain.

Keith Smith

Keith Smith I studied at Harrow School from 1968-70. I have been working at Otterton since 1979. My workshop is in the courtyard of Otterton Mill, the last working water mill on the River Otter. I make ash glazed reduced stoneware, fired in a gas kiln. Most of my work is functional and food orientated. I prefer not to make sets of things, allowing a gradual evolution of shapes to maintain my interest. Full member of the Devon Guild of Craftsmen, and the Somerset Guild of Craftsmen. (Photography - Stephen Hobson)

Mark Smith

Mark Smith Trained at Derby University 1990-92. My speciality is wood-fired saltglaze ceramics for both decorative and functional use. All work is hand thrown on a continental momentum wheel and once fired to a temperature of 1300°C. My forms aim to combine the soft nature of clay and the unpredictable way the flames pass through the chamber of the kiln. Exhibits and sells to galleries in the UK.

John Solly Fellow

John Solly Born Maidstone, Kent 1928. Studied Maidstone, Camberwell and Central Schools of Art. Short working periods with Walter Cole at Rye Pottery, and Ray Finch at Winchcombe Pottery. Established own workshop in Maidstone 1953. Since 1960 has run a regular summer school at the pottery. 1986 moved to Peasmarsh. Still making slipware and high fired earthenware. A founder member of the Craft Potters Association. First Chairman of Kent Potters Association. Fellow Society of Designer-Craftsmen. Member Rye Society of Artists. 1983 invited to run slipware workshop, Middletown, CT, USA. 1989 slipware seminar, Bussum, Holland. 1993 visiting lecturer, La Trobe University, Bendigo, Australia.

Charles Spacey

CS.

Charles Spacey Born in North Wales. Studied ceramics at Farnham (1972-75). Worked as assistant in various workshops both in UK and Continent. Started first workshop in 1979 with Brigitte Spacey in Switzerland . Moved to present workshop near Welshpool, Mid-Wales in 1993. Work is mainly slab built stoneware, comprising teapots, plates and vases. These are decorated during the glazing process with geometrically and visually illusory inspired patterns. Pieces fired to 1300°C in a reducing atmosphere. Has exhibited widely on Continent including Faenza and Vallauris, the UK and Japan.

Chris Speyer Fellow

YERJA

Chris Speyer Trained as a theatre designer and worked in theatre for many years. Now, as the ceramic half of Yerja Ceramics & Textiles, makes thrown and press-moulded stoneware. Work exhibited and sold throughout the UK and abroad.

Rupert Spira

RS

Rupert Spira was born in 1960. He studied under Henry Hammond at West Surrey College of Art and trained with Michael Cardew at Wenford Bridge. He set up Froyle Pottery in Hampshire in 1983, where he worked until 1996, when he moved home and workshop to Shropshire. His work is thrown in stoneware clay, and glazed in a variety of colours. All his pots are made to be used in an everyday way - bowls, cups and saucers, plates, vases, beakers - whether one-off pieces or sets, but their function is not limited by their usefulness.

Christel Spriet

Christel Spriet I studied ceramics at Sint-Lucas Institute for Fine Art in Gent, Belgium. I make stoneware vessels and wall sculptures combining drift-wood, corroded metal and ceramics. I use clay as a medium to pull the whole piece together. Different layers of oxide underglaze enamels, slips and glazes are used to achieve the final result.

Peter Stoodley Fellow

Peter Stoodley makes unglazed inlaid slip decorated planters, sometimes with applied strips, fired in an electric kiln. Studied painting at Bournemouth and Goldsmiths' Schools of Art. During Art Teachers Diploma chose pottery as craft subject at Camberwell. Returned to Bournemouth in 1951 and remained as lecturer until 1980. Set up first workshop in 1952 and began making plant pots to commission. Moved to Lymington in 1987 into larger workshop with additional gas fired kiln. Still makes planters to order or for exhibition but seeks to do more throwing and to return to using glazes on smaller handbuilt pots.

Harry Horlock-Stringer Fellow

Harry Horlock-Stringer One of the 1950s wave of 'Painter turned Potter' who had to teach themselves, he found a new way of understanding the formulation and making of glazes without resort to the use of molecular formulae. Always very interested in teaching, he built a school, literally with his bare hands. This was opened in 1965 and has catered for a large international summer school ever since. An interest in raku in the late fifties led to the first book on the subject to be written in the West in 1967, also designing and making an electric raku kiln safe enough to use in the classroom in 1965. Being confined to the use of electricity only, much research has gone into the development of quality in oxidising atmospheres, this led to the discovery of the first 'Reactive Slip' in 1975. Served for nine years on the Council of the Craft Potters Association during its formative years and was Editor of their journal for a number of years. He continues to contribute to potters' journals. In the fifties he had a workshop in the old Fulham Pottery making once-fired earthenware for domestic use later transferring to Taggs Yard where twice-fired earthenware was made. At present stoneware and a small amount of porcelain, mostly for domestic use is produced. Work has been exhibited in a number of different countries where it is in museums and private collections. He was head of an art department in a Teacher Training College for many years and lectures at home and abroad by invitation.

Helen Swain Fellow

HS ⁹⁷

Helen Swain At present making burnished earthenware. After studying painting, pottery and modelling, I worked with Harry and May Davis in Cornwall. Then three years at Royal Doulton (Lambeth) with Agnete Hoy, carving and painting saltglazed stoneware. From 1963-93 I taught at Goldsmiths' College (London) in the fine ceramic department (now so short-sightedly closed). I had a solus exhibition at CPA in 1961 and have contributed to sixteen groups since then.

Taja

Taja

Taja I was born in Japan and stayed there until my early twenties. Around that time I was learning to oil paint in Kyoto where I met Penny Simpson (whom I later married). She invited me to come to England. I always wanted to see lots of good oil paintings in Europe, so I decided to come . The discovery of Paul Gauguin was a big thing. I learned lots from his composition of colours and shapes. The use of colours in my work is still greatly influenced by him. The first thing I did when I came here apart from painting and drawing was to help Penny in her pottery. She had a spare wheel so I started throwing pots under her supervision. The way I develop my work always comes from the texture of clay. So the most important thing is to emphasise the texture; the less you touch clay the better. That is why I like using the method of slab building, using slabs of clay like paper.Because of the limited shapes I can make using my method sometimes brings me interesting shapes of pots. Then I get inspired by that shape and make new work. So my pots never come from outside of the workshop. I never do drawings of what I want to make. In a way I draw with clay.

Sutton Taylor Fellow

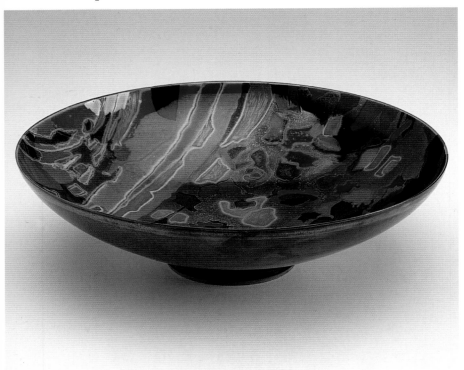

Sutton Taylor was born in Yorkshire and now lives and works in West Cornwall. He exhibits world wide and his work is included in many major collections. The work is richly colourful - he uses a wide palette of colour derived from glazes containing precious metals (gold, silver, copper, platinum and Tantalum) fired under reduction. His forms are mainly vessel shaped but include wall panels and sculptural pieces. Sutton Taylor is represented exclusively by the Hart Gallery where his work is always available.

Sabina Teuteberg Fellow

Sabina Teuteberg studio was first established in 1982. To make her tableware range and one-off pieces she has developed a unique method. Each piece is decorated before forming. Thin layers of coloured clays are rolled onto a base slab, which is then shaped in or over plaster moulds. The industrial method of jigger and jolley has been adapted to suit this personal technique. Since 1990 public art and private commissions have allowed her to work on a large scale. For most projects hand made ceramic components were designed, made and used in combination with industrially made tiles for floors, wall panels and seating. Examples of work in public collections: University of Wales, Cleveland County Museum Service, Ulster Museum, Liverpool Museum and the Crafts Council.

Lyndon Thomas

Lyndon Thomas Born 1941. I have received no formal training in pottery, the skills being accumulated by means of voracious reading and endless practice. In 1967 I set up my first workshop and supply work to various craft outlets. All work is thrown with functional shapes predominating; I obtain greatest satisfaction from making jugs, storage jars and shallow bowls. The bulk of production is oxidised stoneware fired to a maximum temperature of 1270°C in a 12 cu.ft. electric kiln. The clay is grogged stoneware produced by Spencroft, suitable for large and small scale work. Glazes are developed from various recipes with iron being the main colourant.

Owen Thorpe Fellow

Owen Thorpe started pottery in London in 1970 moving to Shropshire in 1975 and Churchstoke, Powys in 1981. Works alone. Produces a range of domestic stoneware using coloured and local clay slips and wax-resist decoration. All work is wheel thrown and is fired with electric oxidising firing. Also produces a range of garden pottery decorated using coloured slip decoration. Also makes highly decorated individual pieces using a technique like majolica but at stoneware temperatures. Tin glazes are employed, some tinted cream or light blue, with elaborate brushed patterns applied to the unfired glaze. This process is also employed in producing 'celebration' ware for anniversaries, presentations, weddings etc., in which majolica decoration is combined with calligraphy. Recent work tending to be more sculptural, based on horse images and figurework.

Anna Timlett

Anna Timlett.

Anna Timlett trained at Cornwall College of Further and Higher Education 1982-84. The pottery was established in 1987 and is one of several workshops in the grounds of a working wool museum. The pots are sold through galleries, exhibitions and the showroom connected to the workshop. The large range of tableware is wheel thrown in repeated designs using a local red earthenware clay; dipped in a white slip and decorated with coloured slips and oxides. After the initial biscuit firing, a clear glaze is applied and fired to 1060°C in an electric kiln. (Photography - Sam Bailey)

Judy Trim Fellow

Judy Trim Born Cambridge. Trained Bath Academy of Art. Lecturer: Central St. Martins, Belfast School of Art, Wimbledon School of Art, Bath Academy of Art. Work in private and public collections: Crafts Council, Shipley Art Gallery, Fitzwilliam Museum, Norwich Museum, Auckland Art Gallery, Los Angeles County Museum. Individual handbuilt coiled pieces using earthenware or T-material, incorporating coloured slips, lustres, smoking and sgraffito.

Katrina Trinick

Katrina Trinick Born in Cornwall 1950. Dip.A.D. Ceramics at Central School of Art and Design, London, 1969-72. Most of my work is handbuilt - coiled, pinched and press-moulded, in a white body which, after biscuit firing in an electric kiln, is smoked in sawdust. This produces random cloud-like patterns in shades of grey and brown through to black. The smoking and the feel of the burnished surface suits the organic forms inspired by shells, pebbles and fossils. Thrown bowls are carved with fossil and shell designs. The scale of work ranges from small pots to large coiled vessels.

Ruthanne Tudball Fellow

Ruthanne Tudball Born in California, USA. Post-graduate Diploma in Ceramics from Goldsmiths' College after years of being mainly self-taught and after gaining an honours degree in English and a Post-Graduate Certificate in Education. All my work is stoneware, raw glazed, slip decorated and once-fired soda-glazed with sodium compounds other than salt. My main concern is with the clay and the pleasure of manipulating it during throwing. I want to make forms that capture the soft plasticity of the material and have both dignity and a lively freshness. Soda glazing can have dramatic effects on the surfaces of the pots emphasizing the making process and path of the flames across the work, rendering each pot unique. I make my pots to be lived with, handled and used.

Sue Varley

SV

Sue Varley I studied at the Bath Academy of Art, Corsham, where I specialised in ceramics and was taught by James Tower. All my work is handbuilt and I make pinched or coiled bowls and pots, using coloured and/or textured clays. The starting point for much of my work is based on drawings, paintings and collages I make, mainly of landscape. At present all my work is fired to earthenware temperatures in an electric kiln. After this initial firing the work is then part-reduced in a brick kiln using sawdust, leaves or newspaper.

Tina Vlassopulos Fellow

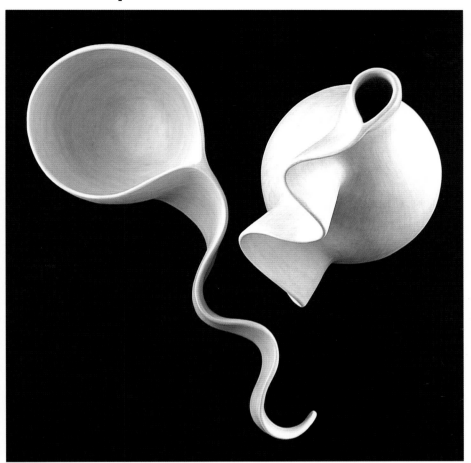

Tina Vlassopulos Individual pieces made from burnished red earthenware or coloured clays.

Edmund de Waal Fellow

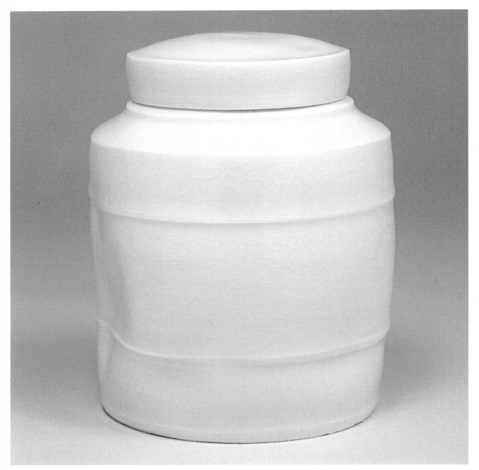

Edmund de Waal makes porcelain vessels: beakers, teapots and large lidded jars.

Carol Wainwright

Carol Wainwright Processes are important. Shredded clays are weathered prior to mixing. Work is thrown and assembled whilst soft - allowing subtle manipulation of shape. The pots are brushed (after biscuiting) with coloured glazes and vitreous slips. The layering and brushing, with thin areas of glaze soaking into the underlying slips during firing, builds a very varied surface. The larger pots and jugs have anthropomorphic connotations and all the work is rooted in contemporary evidence of cultural history - mud granaries, hill-fort landscapes, Han dynasty tomb-ware, Haniwa pots. Much of the work also happens to be functional. Training - Painting at Harrow, late 50s, Ceramics at Farnham, late 70s.

Josie Walter Fellow

Walter.

Josie Walter Born 1951. Trained as an anthropologist, then as a teacher, and finally as a potter on the Studio Ceramics Course, Chesterfield College of Art 1976-79. Spent an invaluable six months as a repetition thrower with Suzie and Nigel Atkins, Poterie du Don, Auvergne, France. Shared a workshop with John Gibson for eight years and then moved to an old mill for the next ten. The workshop has now been relocated in the garden next to the house. Over the past few years I have experimented with cut and torn paper resist, colour infill and slip trailing. Recent pots have explored the qualities inherent in my materials, pouring slips thinly to create overlapping layers and to let the earthenware body show through, or applied thickly with large brushes to wrap the slip around the pots. Using the marks of the brush highlighted with sgraffito has created a greater sense of movement and a fresh perspective. All the work is once fired and to cone 03.

Sarah Walton Fellow

Sarah Walton initially studied painting (1960-64) finding landscape was her chosen subject matter, On discovering that three dimensions interested her more than two she then trained to be a studio potter at Harrow (1971-73). In the following 23 years she has produced firstly thrown tableware and then handbuilt forms for outdoors - all saltglazed. Currently she makes a small square birdbath on a square wood base which evolved from her interest in landscape and natural light. She also makes tiles. The glazed surface of both describe the path of the flame and flux during their firing and are suggestive of stone and moss.

John Ward Fellow

John Ward Born in London 1938. Studied ceramics at Camberwell School of Arts and Crafts (1966-70). Set up first workroom in 1970 and taught part-time at an adult education institute until 1979 before moving to Wales to pot full-time. Central theme is simple hollow forms, often derived from the bowl. Pots are fired in an electric kiln - biscuit fired to 1000°C, glaze 1250°C, but recently some have been once fired to 1250°C using slip glazes. All glazes are matt and are applied by spraying, pouring and painting. Colours mainly used are; black, white, blue/green, ochre and blue.

Sasha Wardell Fellow

Sasha Wardell Born 1956 in Sri Lanka. Studied ceramics at Bath Academy of Art (1976-79). North Staffordshire Polytechnic (1979-81) and Ecole Nationale d'Art Decoratifs in Limoges, France. Has taught in various art colleges since 1981 and set up workshop, exhibiting mainly in the UK and abroad since 1982. Materials and processes involve slipcasting bone china to an egg-shell thinness to enhance translucency. Models are produced by plaster-forming techniques using a turning lathe and hand-carving. After moulding, the pieces are fired three times. This includes a soft-firing, after which the work is sanded, a 1260°C firing to mature the body, and finally, a 1080°C firing to harden on the decoration, which is airbrushed through a series of intricate masks. Author of book - *Slipcasting*, published 1997, A&C Black.

Andrew Watts

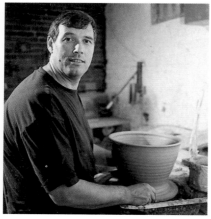

Andrew Watts trained at Camberwell School of Art and opened his first pottery in Battersea, London in 1976. There he made slip-decorated earthenwares. In 1981 he moved to Weston in north Hertfordshire and established Lannock Pottery. Here he makes stonewares of all sorts; useful and decorative; commissioned and individual pieces.

Nicola Werner

Nicola Werner After an invaluable training with Alan Caiger-Smith at Aldermaston Pottery, Nicola Werner set up her own pottery in 1986 in Kent, moved to Somerset in 1987 and established her present larger workshop in Devon in 1992. The pots are thrown in Fremington red earthenware, biscuit-fired, dipped in a white tin glaze and painted with birds, flowers, leaves etc. in the European tradition. She is much influenced by old majolica, Faience and Delftware. She travels when possible for new inspiration, whilst working within the structure of producing a reliable range of domestic ware, commemorative pieces and tile commissions. The pots are available from the workshop, at selected galleries or by mail order.

Gilda Westermann

gW

Gilda Westermann I make a range of white porcelain tableware and one-off pieces. Simplicity and balance of shape are the prime criteria of my work. A wide selection of shells build the basic 'alphabet' for my decorations.

John Wheeldon Fellow

John Wheeldon Trained at Chesterfield College of Art and Wolverhampton Polytechnic 1969-71. Having been involved with the production of basalt and porcelain pots decorated with precious metal lustres for several years I am increasingly becoming more involved in raku. I especially love the rich velvety blacks of the smoked body and the contrast they produce with the glaze and slips. Whilst still producing the lustreware I envisage greater exploration of the raku and low-fire techniques in the next few years. Presently I am potter-in-residence at Repton School and a Council Member of the CPA. I have recently moved from my previous address to a house in the centre of the village where I have a large gallery showing both my own and other potters' work.

Rob Whelpton

Rob Whelpton studied ceramics at North Staffordshire Polytechnic 1971-74. After college worked in Botswana and then lived in Denmark from 1975-83, though not potting. Returned to England in 1983 and worked as trainee at Dart Pottery until 1985 when established workshop with wife Vicky. Rob makes raku fired pots using a T-material type body which are decorated with fish, bird and animal motifs drawn onto the pots while leatherhard. They are then coloured using slips and metalic salts. Some pots are enhanced using gold leaf.

David White Fellow

David White My work is predominantly crackle glazed porcelain. I have produced a wide range of glazes which craze in various ways. The glazes are then blended by carefully controlled spraying, using up to five glazes on a pot. On cooling the pots are coated with a carbon based ink and washed off immediately. By doing perpetual tests and experiments and copious notes of how the pots were glazed, a degree of control on the crazing can be achieved. Almost 50% out of each firing are considered unsatisfactory and are reglazed and refired.

David Constantine White

David Constantine White A constantly changing range of decorative domestic earthenware from local clays keeps me up late and out of the pub.

Mary White Fellow

Mary White Trained at Newport School of Art, Hammersmith School of Art and Goldsmiths' College. Initiated the Ceramic Workshop in Atlantic College 1962-72, then set up own workshop. With my husband Charles, moved into wine-producing village in S.W. Germany in 1980 to be in the middle of Europe. Was awarded the State Prize for Ceramic in 1982, then other prizes internationally. I have exhibited all over Europe and USA and was proud to have work shown in the Musee des Arts Decoratifs, Louvre, Paris. My work is in many international collections and museums and is represented in numerous international books, magazines and catalogues. My newest work uses coloured inlays (porcelain). I am also a professional calligrapher and now integrate letters in clay forms. I give lectures and workshops on Letters and Clay in Germany and USA.

Tony White

TW

Tony White established his present workshop at Cwmystwyth, Ceredigion in 1990 and since then all his work has been fired using the raku process. He likes variety in his work, which includes throwing and extruding forms, though he mainly produces animal figures which are slab built with T material; these include Indian runner ducks, dogs, cats, puffins, penguins, chickens and seals. The majority of his work is sold through gallery shops, many on the Crafts Council list, alternatively his work may be purchased direct, by a visit or mail order, please phone for details.

Caroline Whyman Fellow

Caroline Whyman I work with porcelain, attracted initially by its whiteness, which lifts the colour of glazes and makes them sing. I try to throw forms that reach towards subtlety and simplicity, hopefully belying the effort behind working with what is described as 'tricky' clay. Like many porcelain perfectionists I am rarely satisfied with the results. There is a strong thread of connection in the decorated work, based on grids, which I use to create symbolic patterns rooted in geometry and weaving. The designs are carved and inlaid with stained porcelain slips; some boil in the kiln, emerging through the bright glazes as a palpable textured line on the surface. I like to work on themes, making one-off pieces, or small batches which allow me to change and develop my work as new ideas arise.

Maggie Williams

Maggie Williams makes individual thrown and handbuilt ceramics in stoneware and porcelain. Born 1952. Studied Foundation at St. Albans (1971-72), Graphic Design at Canterbury ('72-'75) and Ceramics at Medway ('81-'84) with Peter Phillips, Geoffery Whiting and Colin Pearson. Studio based in Faversham since '84. Subject leader for Ceramics B.A. courses at Canterbury Christ Church College since '91.The work is mainly vessel based, concerned with form, balance and asymmetry and often the relationship between forms. Experimenting with surface and glaze is also a constant fascination. Commissions have been undertaken for larger scale work, and for design companies and television. Work is mainly sold through galleries and exhibitions.

Peter Wills

Peter Wills Inspiration for me comes from simple things; pots from ancient China to modern Europe; the looseness, freedom and life of Bizen wares; the wonderful colours and textures of Rie; the blackbird singing outside my bedroom window each morning. I work in a tiny studio with white clay bodies which I blend to my own recipes. All pots are thrown on a home built kick/electric wheel, raw glazed and fired to Orton cone 9 (1290°C). I aim for balanced form, attention to detail and heart. My desire to produce pots of a calibre that will make people catch their breath; but for now if I can occasionally stir the heart I'll be content.

George Wilson

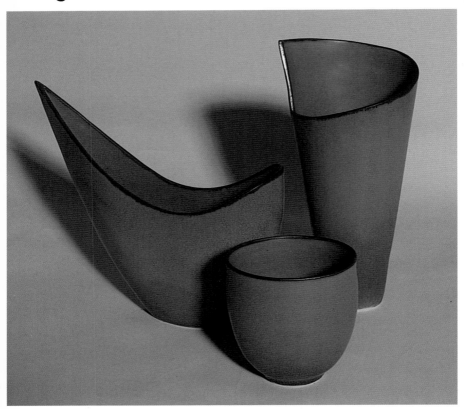

George Wilson

George Wilson took early retirement from full-time teaching at the Richmond Adult College (where he was the founder of the Ceramics Department) in order to devote more time to producing his own work in his Ealing, West London studio. He continues to teach part-time at Brunel University and Surbiton College. He works mainly in reduction and oxidised stoneware and in lustred porcelain, producing individual decorative pieces for interior designers and architects, and containers for Ikebana flower arranging. George exhibits widely in the UK and sells work in America and Europe. He aims to have at least one major solus exhibition a year. He is currently designing and producing a range of pottery exclusive to leading London stores.

David Winkley Fellow

VELLOW
Somerset

David Winkley Born in Lancashire in 1939. Trained initially as a painter at the School of Fine Art, Reading University and Pembroke College, Cambridge. Began making pots with the late Bernard Forrester at Dartington in 1963. Opened his first workshop in Bristol the following year. Since 1966 has been at his present pottery where he makes a particularly wide range of stoneware pots for everyday use together with individual pieces in stoneware and porcelain. Firings are in a 230 cu.ft. two-chamber oil-fired kiln.

Mary Wondrausch Fellow

Mary Wondrausch I work in earthenware using a honey glaze for the the more traditional slip-trailed pots. I specialize in individually commissioned commemorative plates, which customers are able to collect from the workshop, converted from an eighteenth century stable in a magical setting. These can also be posted worldwide. The subject of my gouache paintings is often reflected in the central decoration of the large cheese platters (see illustration). Latterly I have been developing a more painterly style with sgraffito fish and bird motifs using painted slips as well as oxides. My work is predominately functional, rather than sculptural.

Gary Wood Fellow

Gary Wood The work is all to do with giving presence to form, causing resonance, making something possible. I make huge bowls, vases, stools. Table landscapes: pots for food and drink. I also make sculptural form: monuments, diaries, shrines and totems. I use several slips and glazes in combination to create a depth of surface which reveals wet and dry qualities on the same piece by pairing matt and glossy glazes with reactive slips. Colour comes from black copper oxide and zinc - a range between delicate frosty mint green to crystal white, satin grey to rich matt black. Dolomite will add subtle flesh tones, highlights, edges. Born in Bradford, West Yorkshire 1955. Studied at Cumbria College of Art and Design, Carlisle 1984-86. Winner of Northern Arts Craft Award and Northern Arts Travel Award. Recent exhibitions at South Hill Park Arts Centre, Bracknell; Country Works Gallery, Montgomery; Black Swan Guild, Frome; Rye Art Gallery, Sussex; T. Garner Gallery, Glasgow; Anderson Gallery, Worcestershire. Forthcoming shows at Contemporary Ceramics (In the Window), London, August 97, Rufford Craft Centre, Nottinghamshire, November 97-January 98. (Photography - John Chalice)

Karen Ann Wood Fellow

Karen Ann Wood makes a range of table and ovenware - some oxidised, some reduced - in a gas fired kiln. Currently has an especial interest in shino-type glazes. Trained in Canada, New Zealand and the UK after gaining a B.A. from the University of Western Australia. Teaches ceramics part-time and has worked from the same studio since 1978.

Steve Woodhead Fellow

Steve Woodhead I have been potting for 17 years and have made a variety of functional decorative pieces based on traditional forms. I am now pursuing pots that are more individual in nature, incorporating more flamboyant shapes and vibrant colours.

Rosemary Wren Honorary Fellow **and Peter Crotty**

Rosemary Wren and Peter Crotty Rosemary Wren is still making her stoneware animals and birds by traditional pot-making techniques, but instead of outlining the colour shapes by incising into smooth surface, the pattern is derived from a new method of building. This uses thumbfuls of clay and curled up coils of clay to construct hollow forms, with added tiny coils beaten into the surface. Form and pattern are integrated by brushing in and sponging off superimposed layers of colour, infilling the crevices and crannies. Rosemary is also making free-standing landscapes in the same way, feeling for the characteristics of form that give a sense of place, as she does for the shapes of her creatures. (Photography - Marshall Anderson)

Gill Wright

Gill Wright works in red earthenware and makes handbuilt pots which are burnished and sawdust fired.

Takeshi Yasuda Fellow

Takeshi Yasuda was trained at Daisei Pottery in Mashiko, Japan (1963-65). Worked in UK since 1973. Exhibits widely and has work in public and private collections abroad and in the UK, including the Victoria and Albert Museum. Currently Professor of Applied Art at University of Ulster in Belfast, and tutor at the Royal College of Art, London.

Joanna and Andrew Young Fellows

A & J YOUNG   GRESHAM

Joanna and Andrew Young Dip. A.D. Ceramics at W.S.C.A.D. Farnham, Surrey, 1970-73. Worked in France with Gwyn Hanssen for six months, A.T.C. Goldsmiths' College, London 1974. Set up workshop 1975 in Hunworth, North Norfolk. Interest was, and still is, to provide interesting and practical everyday pots in a repeated range. Most pots are wheel thrown, some are shaped later by cutting and squaring in various ways. The main glaze is thinly applied, and once fired under reduction in a 100 cu.ft. gas kiln. The finish is often mistaken for saltglaze. 1981, moved to large workshop at Lower Gresham, Norfolk. Continued production with two assistants. The pots are sold to some shops and also through own shop next door to workshop. Occasional exhibitions, Crafts Council Bursary 1988. Now making white stoneware with mainly dark shiny green glaze and more decoration.

VISITING A POTTER

This is a full list of names and addresses of fellows and professional members of the CPA, together with details of opening hours. For approximate locations refer to the map on page 340.

1
Adrian Abberley   *Fellow*
95a Sheen Road
Richmond-upon-Thames
Surrey TW9 1YJ
(0181) 948 1234
Please telephone

2
Billy Adams   *Fellow*
39 Cosmeston Street
Cathays
Cardiff
CF2 4LQ
(01222) 668998
Visitors welcome but please telephone first

3
David Allnatt
3 Poplar Gardens
Napton On The Hill
Warwickshire CV23 8NT
(01926) 813438
Visitors welcome by appointment only

4
Marilyn Andreetti
Belle Vue
16 Gews Corner
Cheshunt
Herts EN8 9BX
(01992) 639969
Visitors welcome but please telephone first

5
Tim Andrews   *Fellow*
Woodbury Pottery
Greenway
Woodbury
Exeter
Devon EX5 1LW
(01392) 233475
Showroom usually open Mon-Sat 10am-6pm, but it is advisable to telephone if making special journey

6
Mick Arnup   *Fellow*
Holtby Pottery
Holtby
York YO1 3UA
(01904) 489377
Showroom open 10.00-18.00 every day. Holtby is five miles from York on A166

7
Keith Ashley   *Fellow*
The Chocolate Factory
Farleigh Place
Stoke Newington
London N16 7SX
(0171) 503 7896
Visitors welcome but please telephone first

8
Chris Aston   *Fellow*
Chris Aston Pottery
High Street
Elkesley
nr. Retford
Nottinghamshire DN22 8AJ
Tel/Fax (01777) 838 391
E-mail chris-aston-ceramics@compuserve.com
The village of Elkesley, once part of the estates belonging to the Dukes of Newcastle on the edge of Sherwood Forest, is on the A1, 20 miles north of Newark and only 20 minutes drive from Rufford. Visitors are always welcome to the workshop and gallery showroom, generally open 7 days a week, 10am to 6pm. Please phone beforehand if coming from a long distance

9
Angela Atkinson
86 London Road
Newcastle Under Lyme
Staffordshire ST5 1LZ
(01782) 634618

10
Felicity Aylieff   *Fellow*
37 Kensington Gardens
Bath BA1 6LH
Tel. (01225) 334136
Fax. (01225) 313492
Visitors welcome but by appointment only

11
Elizabeth Aylmer
Widgery House
20 Market Street
Hatherleigh
Devon EX20 3JP

(01837) 810624

Shop and Showroom open daily, but please
telephone out of season

12
Duncan Ayscough
'Farmers'
Bethlehem
Carmarthenshire SA19 9DW

(01550) 777 460

Visitors by appointment only

13
Sylph Baier
Tin Star Studio
38 Cheltenham Place
Brighton
Sussex BN1 4AB

(01273) 682042

Visitors are welcome by appointment

14
Chris Barnes
Unit 3
The Chocolate Factory
Farleigh Place
Stoke Newington
London N16 7SX

(0171) 503 6961

Visitors are welcome, best to ring first

15
Richard Baxter
Old Leigh Studios
61 High Street
Leigh-on-Sea
Essex SS9 2EP

(01702) 470490

Open Tuesday-Sunday 11am-5pm Closed Monday

16
Svend Bayer   *Fellow*
Duckpool Cottage
Sheepwash
Beaworthy
Devon EX21 5PW

(01409) 231282

Pottery always open. Visitors welcome but best to
telephone first

17
Deborah Baynes
Nether Hall
Shotley
Ipswich
Suffolk IP9 1PW

(01473) 788300
Fax: (01473) 787055

Visitors very welcome but please telephone first

18
Peter Beard   *Fellow*
Tanners Cottage
Welsh Road
Cubbington
Leamington Spa
Warwickshire CV32 7UB

Tel/Fax: (01926) 428481

Studio open at any reasonable time. Visitors very
welcome but must make an appointment

19
John Bedding
1 Lower Fish Street
St. Ives
Cornwall TR26 1LT

(01736) 794930
Fax: (01736) 796324

Showroom Gallery open weekdays and Saturday

20
Beverley Bell-Hughes   *Fellow*
Fron Dirion
Conwy Road
Llandudno Junction
Gwynedd LL31 9AY

(01492) 572575

Visitors by appointment only

21
Terry Bell-Hughes   *Fellow*
Fron Dirion
Conwy Road
Llandudno Junction
Gwynedd LL31 9AY

(01492) 572575

Visitors by appointment only

22
Julian Bellmont
24 High Street
Kintbury
Hungerford
Berkshire RG17 9TW

(01488) 657388
Email: pottery@jbellmont.demon.co.uk

Website: www.jbellmont.demon.co.uk

Visitors are welcome to the showroom 9am-
5.30pm, Tuesdays to Saturdays

23
Kochevet Ben-David   *Fellow*
147 Overhill Road
London SE22 0PT

Tel/Fax: (0181) 516 1241
Email: S.H.Walker@gre.ac.uk

Visitors welcome, please telephone first

24
Suzanne Bergne   *Fellow*
Cambrays Barn
Upper Slaughter
Gloucestershire GL54 2JB

(01451) 821328
Fax: (01451) 820610

Visitors are welcome to see work at the studio.
Please make a prior appointment

25
Maggie Angus Berkowitz   *Fellow*
21-23 Park Road
Milnthorpe
Cumbria LA7 7AD

Tel/Fax: (015395) 63970
Email: maggie@kencomp.net
work on: http://www.bigfish.co.uk/mab/
and on: http://www.lmu.ac.uk/ces/axis

Welcomes visitors by appointment

26
John Berry   *Fellow*
45 Chancery Lane
Beckenham
Kent BR3 2NR

(0181) 658 0351

27
David Binns
10 Parc-y-Llan
Cilcain
Mold
Flintshire
North Wales CN7 5NF

(01352) 741256 (Home)
(01772) 893384 (Work)
Email: d.s.binns@uclan.ac.uk

Visitors welcome by prior appointment

28
Gillian Bliss
32 Talbot Street
Canton
Cardiff CF1 9BW

(01222) 373626

Visitors by appointment only please

29
Keith Booth
100 King Edward Road
Maidstone
Kent ME15 6PL

(01622) 683816

Visitors by appointment only

30
Martin Booth
Unit 11
Townhouse Studios
Alsager Road
Audley
Stoke-on-Trent
Staffordshire ST7 8JQ

(01782) 720982

31
Richard Boswell
66 Wallington Shore Road
Wallington
Fareham
Hampshire PO16 8SJ

(01329) 511497

Visitors by appointment please

32
Clive Bowen *Fellow*
Shebbear Pottery
Shebbear
Beaworthy
Devon EX21 5QZ
(01409) 281271
Wholesale and retail customers are welcome at
the showroom

33
Loretta Braganza *Fellow*
The Coach House
198 Mount Vale
York YO2 2DL
(01904) 630454
Visitors by appointment only

34
Carlo Briscoe & Edward Dunn *Fellows*
Gwaith Menyn
Llanglydwen
Whitland
Dyfed SA34 0XP
Tel/Fax (01994) 419402
Visitors welcome but please telephone first

35
David Brown
Highway Cottage
Church Street
Merriott
Somerset TA16 5PR
(01460) 75655
Visitors welcome by appointment

36
Sandy Brown *Fellow*
Anchorage
3 Marine Parade
Appledore
Bideford
Devon EX39 1PJ
(01237) 478219
Visitors very welcome. Take a chance or ring first
to make sure

37
Jenny Browne
Shaftesbury Studios
47 Tyneham Road
London SW11 5XH
(0171) 228 0804
Visitors by appointment please

38
Susan Bruce
4 Pinewood
Woodbridge
Suffolk IP12 4DS
(01394) 384865
Visitors welcome but telephone first

39
Karen Bunting
53 Beck Road
London E8 4RE
(0171) 249 3016
Visitors welcome by appointment

40
Jan Bunyan
4 Bridge Road
Butlers Marston
Warwick CV35 0NE
(01926) 741560
Small showroom: Visitors welcome but advisable
to telephone first

41
Deirdre Burnett *Fellow*
Kilnyard Cottage
48 Gipsy Hill
London SE19 1NL
(0181) 670 6565

42
Ian Byers *Fellow*
16 Stroud Road
South Norwood
London SE25 5DR
(0181) 654 0225
Visitors welcome by appointment

43
John Calver *Fellow*
23 Silverdale Road
Yealand Redmayne
Carnforth
Lancs. LA5 9TA
(01524) 781362
Visitors are welcome to the workshop but please
telephone first

44
Kyra Cane
41 Westhill Drive
Mansfield
Nottinghamshire NG18 1PL

(01623) 20815

Visitors welcome, telephone first

45
Seth Cardew   *Fellow*
Wenford Bridge Pottery
St. Breward
Bodmin
Cornwall PL30 3PN

(01208) 850471

Visitors welcome by appointment

46
Daphne Carnegy   *Fellow*
Kingsgate Workshops
110-116 Kingsgate Road
London NW6 2JG

(0171) 328 2051
Fax: (0171) 328 7878

Visitors welcome by appointment

47
Tony Carter
Low Road
Debenham
Stowmarket
Suffolk IP14 6QU

(01728) 860475
Fax: (01728) 861110

Pottery and Shop open to public all year round

48
Michael Casson   *Honorary Fellow*
Wobage Farm
Upton Bishop
Ross-on-Wye
Herefordshire HR9 7QP

(01989) 780 233

Showroom open 10am-5pm on Saturdays and
Sundays. Other times please telephone first

49
Sheila Casson   *Fellow*
Wobage Farm
Upton Bishop
Ross-on-Wye
Herefordshire HR9 7QP

(01989) 780 233

Showroom open 10am-5pm on Saturdays and
Sundays. Other times please telephone first

50
Trevor Chaplin
Marridge Hill Cottage
Ramsbury
Marlborough
Wiltshire SN8 2HG

(01672) 520486

Visitors welcome but please telephone first

51
Richard Charters
Harehope Forge Pottery
Harehope Farm
Eglingham
Alnwick
Northumberland NE66 2DW

(01668) 217347
Fax: (01665) 510624
Email richard@tag.co.uk
Web www.tag.co.uk/harehope

52
Linda Chew   *Fellow*
42 Cheriton Road
Winchester
Hampshire SO22 5AY

(01962) 867218

Visitors welcome but please telephone first

53
Derek Clarkson   *Fellow*
1 The Poplars
Bacup
Lancashire OL13 8AD

(01706) 874541

Visitors welcome, telephone first if possible

54
Margery Clinton   *Fellow*
2 Templelands
29 High Street
Dunbar
East Lothian EH42 1EN

(01368) 865522

Visitors welcome by appointment

55
Peter Clough   *Fellow*
34 Dragon View
Harrogate
N. Yorkshire HG1 4DG

(01423) 506700 (Home)
(01904) 616714 (Work)

Visitors by prior arrangement only

56
Desmond Clover
Clover Pottery
5 Oldhurst Road
Pidley
Huntingdon
Cambs PE17 3BY

(01487) 841 026

Shop open most days, if travelling any distance, please telephone first

57
Russell Coates   *Fellow*
10 The Butts
Frome
Somerset BA11 4AA

(01373) 452443

Visitors welcome but please telephone first

58
Rosemary Cochrane
Pen-y-Stair Farm
Mamhilad
Pontypool
Gwent NP4 8RG

(01873) 880696

Visitors welcome but please telephone first

59
Roger Cockram   *Fellow*
Chittlehampton Pottery
Chittlehampton
North Devon EX37 9PX

(01769) 540420

Vistors welcome to showroom. 10-1, 2-5.30 weekdays. Often also weekends, but best telephone first

60
Elaine Coles
The Bank Gallery
73/75 High Street
Chobham
Surrey GU24 8AF

(01276) 857369

Open Tuesday-Saturday 10am-5pm Closed Bank Holidays

61
Nic Collins
Powdermill Pottery
Powdermills
Postbridge
Yelverton
Devon PL20 6SP

(01822) 880263

62
Barbara Colls   *Fellow*
177 Thunder Lane
Thorpe St Andrew
Norwich NR7 0JF

(01603) 436695

No showroom but visitors welcome by appointment

63
Jennifer Colquitt
Field Ceramics
Holloway Chambers
27 Priory Street
Dudley
West Midlands DY1 1EZ

(01384) 455591 (Studio)
(01384) 258522 (Home/answerphone)

Visitors welcome to studio, please telephone first

64
Jo Connell
Witherley Lodge
12 Watling Street
Witherley
Atherstone
Warwickshire CV9 1RD

(01827) 712128

Visitors welcome by appointment

65
Clare Conrad
14 Cambridge Park
Redland
Bristol BS6 6XW

(0117) 924 7001 (Studio)

66
Joanna Constantinidis   *Fellow*
2 Bells Chase
Great Baddow
Chelmsford
Essex CM2 8DT

(01245) 471842

Visitors by appointment only

67
Delan Cookson   *Fellow*
Lissadell
St Buryan
Penzance
Cornwall TR19 6HP

(01736) 810347

Visitors welcome at showroom/workshop by
appointment

68
Bennett Cooper   *Fellow*
Mistley Quay Workshops
Mistley
Manningtree
Essex CO11 1HB

(01206) 393884

Showroom open seven days a week 10am – 6pm

69
Emmanuel Cooper   *Fellow*
Fonthill Pottery
38 Chalcot Road
London NW1 8LP

(0171) 722 9090

Visitors welcome by appointment

70
Gilles Le Corre   *Fellow*
19 Howard Street
Oxford OX4 3AY

(01865) 245 289

Visitors by appointment

71
Jane Cox
85 Wickham Road
Brockley
London SE4 1NH

(0181) 692 6742

Visitors by appointment

72
Molly Curley
32 South Rise
Llanishen
Cardiff CF4 5RH

(01222) 756428

Visitors are welcome by appointment

73
Louise Darby
Clay Barn
Redhill
Alcester
Warwickshire B49 6NQ

(01789) 765214

Visitors welcome but please telephone first for
directions. Some work always on display

74
Dartington Pottery   *Fellows*
Shinners Bridge
Dartington
Totnes
Devon TQ9 6JE

(01803) 864163
Fax: (01803) 864641

Shop opening hours Monday-Saturday 10.00am –
6.00pm

75
Clive Davies   *Fellow*
Valley Barn
Homersfield
Harleston
Norfolk IP20 0NS

(01986) 788144

Visitors welcome to studio but please telephone
first to avoid disappointment

76
Joyce Davison
Chapel House
75 Pales Green
Castle Acre
King's Lynn
Norfolk PE32 2AL

(01760) 755405

Visitors are welcome but please telephone first if
making special journey

77
John Dawson
91 St Johns Wood Terrace
London NW8 6PY

(0171) 722 2698

78
Richard Dewar
Pottery La Rouaudais
44460 Avessac
France

(00 33) 99 91 03 05

79
Peter and Jill Dick *Fellows*
Coxwold Pottery
Coxwold
York YO6 4AA

(01347) 868344

Opening hours 2-5.30 Tuesday-Friday. Also
Sundays from June-August. If you are coming to
see us specially it is wise to 'phone in advance

80
Mike Dodd *Fellow*
Manor Farm
Chedington
Beaminster
Dorset DT8 3HY

(01935) 891225

Please telephone first

81
Jack Doherty *Fellow*
Hooks Cottage
Lea Bailey
Ross-on-Wye
Herefordshire
HR9 5TY

Tel/Fax: (01989) 750644

Visitors are welcome at the workshop and
showroom, please telephone first

82
Karen Downing
29 Andalus Road
London SW9 9PQ

(0171) 326 5197
Fax: (0171) 737 4449

83
Bridget Drakeford
Upper Buckenhill Farmhouse
Fownhope
Hereford HR1 4PU

(01432) 860411

Visitors welcome by appointment

84
John Dunn *Fellow*
Open Studios
168 Kings Road Arches
Brighton,
Sussex BN1 1NB

Tel. (01273) 725013
Fax. (01273) 732626

Visitors welcome by appointment

85
Geoffrey Eastop *Fellow*
The Pottery
Ecchinswell
nr Newbury
Berkshire RG15 8TT

(01635) 298220

Open most days by appointment

86
Victoria and Michael Eden
Parkside
Hale
nr. Milnthorpe
Cumbria LA7 7BL

Tel/Fax: (015395) 62342

Visitors always welcome, but please telephone
first

87
Libby Edmondson
429 Blackburn Road
Higher Wheelton
Chorley
Lancashire PR6 8HY

(01254) 830035

Visitors welcome by appointment

88
Nigel Edmondson
429 Blackburn Road
Higher Wheelton
Chorley
Lancashire PR6 8HY

(01254) 830035

Visitors welcome by appointment

89
Derek Emms *Fellow*
Mossfield Cottage
Hayes Bank
Stone
Staffs. ST15 8SZ

(01785) 812048

Visitors welcome by appointment only

90
James Evans
3 Iliffe Yard
Pullens Estate
London SE17 3QA

(0171) 277 1720

91
Kirsti Buhler Fattorini
5 Broadway
Hale
Cheshire WA15 0PF

(0161) 980 4504

Visitors welcome by appointment

92
Dorothy Feibleman *Fellow*
10 Arlingford Road
London SW2 2SU

(0181) 674 8979

Visitors welcome by appointment

93
Ray Finch *Honorary Fellow*
Winchcombe Pottery
Broadway Road
Winchcombe
Cheltenham
Glos. GL54 5NU

(01242) 602462
Email:
winchcombe_pottery@compuserve.com.uk

Open all year Monday-Friday 9am-5pm Saturday
10am-4pm (Showroom only) May-September
Sunday Noon-4pm (Showroom only)

94
Judith Fisher
Huntswood
St. Helena's Lane
Streat
nr. Hassocks
Sussex BN6 8SD

(01273) 890088

Visitors welcome by appointment

95
Robert Fournier *Fellow*
8 Ladywood
Market Lavington
Devizes
Wiltshire SN10 4DL

(01380) 812342

Built Ducketts Wood Pottery, Heretfordshire 1946
– slipware, tin glaze over slip, mosaics,etc. With
Sheila Fournier, potting in London, at Castle
Hill, Kent, and Lacock, Wiltshire making
stoneware and porcelain. Many slides, films, and
books and, until 1987, the Craft Potters
Association Archives. Retired from potting 1987,
continued with books including, in conjunction
with **Eric Yates-Owen**, *20th Century Studio Potters and
Their Marks*, now underway (1997)

96
Sylvia Des Fours *Fellow*
Heather Hill
Givons Grove
Leatherhead
Surrey KT22 8LB

(01372) 372473

Visitors welcome by appointment

97
Geraldine Fox
83 Green Lane
Coventry
West Midlands CV3 6DN

(01203) 690244

Visitors by appointment

98
David Frith *Fellow*
Brookhouse Pottery & Malt House Gallery
Brookhouse Lane
Denbigh
Denbighshire
Wales LL16 4RE

Tel/Fax: (01745) 812805
Email: D&Mfrith@pottery.demon.co.uk
Web site: www.pottery.demon.co.uk

Gallery and riverside garden open 10am-6pm six
days. Also most Sundays. Phone if coming far

99
Margaret Frith *Fellow*
Brookhouse Pottery & Malt House Gallery
Brookhouse Lane
Denbigh
Denbighshire LL16 4RE

Tel/Fax: (01745) 812805
Email: D&Mfrith@pottery.demon.co.uk
Web site: www.pottery.demon.co.uk

Gallery and riverside garden open 10am-6pm six
days. Also most Sundays. Phone if coming far

100
Tessa Fuchs *Fellow*
24 Cross Road
Kingston-upon-Thames
Surrey KT2 6HG

(0181) 549 6906

Visitors by appointment only

101
Liz Gale   *Fellow*
Taplands Farm Cottage
Webbs Green
High Street
Soberton
Hampshire SO32 3PY

Tel/Fax: (01705) 632686
Email: tonygale@interalpha.co.uk
Visitors welcome but please telephone first

102
Tony Gant   *Fellow*
53 Southdean Gardens
Southfields
London SW19 6NT

(0181) 789 4518

Monday to Saturday 10am-5pm. Please telephone
before calling.

103
Philip Gardiner
8 Fore Street
Mevagissey
nr St. Austell
Cornwall PL26 6UQ

(01726) 842042/844354

The pottery/shop is in the centre of Mevagissey.
Open from Easter to Christmas

104
Jonathan Garratt
Hare Lane Pottery
Cranborne
nr. Wimborne
Dorset BH21 5QT

(01725) 517700

Open Sundays and most other times during week.
Please telephone to check

105
Carolyn Genders   *Fellow*
2 Percy Cottages
London Road
Cuckfield
Sussex RH17 5EP

(01444) 452374

Visitors welcome by prior arrangement

106
Rodney George
Le Jardinet
Klein Cabrierre Street
Franschhoek 7690
South Africa

(00 27) 02212 2186

107
Christine Gittings
Model House Craft & Design Centre
Bull Ring
Lantrisant
Mid Glamorgan CF72 8EB

(01443) 237758

108
Richard Godfrey   *Fellow*
Battisborough House
Holbeton
Nr. Plymouth
South Devon PL8 1JT

(01752) 830457

Visitors are welcome. Please telephone before
8am or after 6pm

109
Nigel Graham
Peartree Designs and Pottery
Rosemount
Muddles Green
Chiddingly
Lewes
East Sussex BN8 6MA

Tel/Fax: (01825) 872246
Mobile (0421) 618374

Visitors always welcome, but please telephone
first

110
Christopher Green   *Fellow*
34 Northover Road
Westbury-on-Trym
Bristol BS9 3LL

(0117) 9500852
cg@seegreen.com

Visitors by appointment

111
Paul Green
Abbey Pottery
Cerne Abbas
Dorchester
Dorset DT2 7JQ

(01300) 341865

Customers always welcome. Showroom open
Tuesday to Sunday 10am-6pm. Closed more
frequently January and February – please phone.

112
Ian Gregory   *Fellow*
The Studio
Crumble Cottage
Ansty, nr. Dorchester
Dorset DT2 7PN

Tel/Fax: (01258) 880891

Workshop and studio open 2.00-6.00pm
weekdays. 9.00am-6.00pm Weekends, or by
arrangement

113
Mark Griffiths   *Fellow*
The Old School
Culmington, nr. Ludlow
Shropshire SY8 2DF

(01584) 861212

Visitors welcome, please telephone first

114
Dimitra Grivellis
6 Broadway Market Mews
London E8 4TS

(0171) 249 5455

Visitors welcome but please telephone first

115
Barry Guppy
Pimlico Pottery
4-6 Moreton Street
Vauxhall Bridge Road
London SW1V 2PS

(0171) 834 7904
Fax: (0171) 834 1423

116
Morgen Hall   *Fellow*
Studio 5
Chapter Arts Centre
Market Road
Canton
Cardiff CF5 1QE

(01222) 396061 ext. 219
(01222) 238716

Visitors always welcome, but please telephone
first

117
Janet Halligan
The Old School
Over Road
Church Minshull
Nantwich
Cheshire CW5 6EA

(01270) 522416

Visitors always welcome but please telephone first

118
Frank Hamer   *Fellow*
Llwyn-On
Croes-yn-y-Pant
Mamhilad
Pontypool NP4 8RE

(01495) 785700

Visitors welcome preferably by appointment

119
Mo Hamid
Star Brewery Pottery
Castle Ditch Lane
Lewes
East Sussex BN7 1YJ

(01273) 483 295

120
Jane Hamlyn   *Fellow*
Millfield Pottery
Everton
nr. Doncaster
S. Yorks DN10 5DD

(01777) 817 723

Visitors welcome – telephone first if possible

298

121
Tracey Handby
25 Perivale Grange
Perivale Lane
Greenford
Middlesex UB6 8TN
(0181) 991 5270

122
Caroline Harvie
Scott's Buildings
Castlehill
Kintore
Aberdeenshire AB51 0UA
(01467) 632583

123
Michael and Barbara Hawkins   *Fellows*
Port Isaac Pottery
Roscarrock Hill
Port Isaac
Cornwall PL29 3RG
Tel/Fax: (01208) 880625
Showroom open all year 10-4. (closed Mondays
in winter). All visitors welcome

124
Peter Hayes   *Fellow*
2 Cleveland Bridge
Bath BA1 5DH
(01225) 466215
Fax: (01225) 311233
Visitors welcome

125
Andrew Hazelton
The Pottery
Aldermaston
Berkshire RG7 4LN
(01734) 713359

126
Alan Heaps   *Fellow*
Minhafren
Aberbechan
Newtown
Powys SY16 3AW
(01686) 630644
Workshop is open at any reasonable time

127
André Hess   *Fellow*
32 Seaman Close
St. Albans
Hertforshire AL2 2NX
Tel/Fax: (01727) 874299
Visitors welcome but please telephone first

128
Karin Hessenberg   *Fellow*
72 Broomgrove Road
Sheffield S10 2NA
(0114) 2661610
128 Robey Street
Sheffield S4 8JG (studio)

129
Elaine Hewitt
Summerhill Cottage
Summerhill Lane
Frensham
Farnham
Surrey GU10 3EN
(01252) 793955
Visitors welcome by appointment

130
John Higgins   *Fellow*
32 Seaman Close
Park Street
St. Albans
Herts. AL2 2NX
(01727) 874299
Visitors welcome by appointment

131
Andrew Hill
Lower Beardshaw Head
Trawden
Colne
Lancashire BB8 8PP
(01282) 866771
Visitors welcome please telephone first

132
John M Hobson
8 Grenville Road
Penylan
Cardiff
South Glamorgan CF2 5BP
(01222) 496817

133
S. J. Holliday
25 Cowl Street
Shepton Mallet
Somerset BA4 5ER

134
Terri Holman
Northcombe
Moretonhampstead Road
Bovey Tracey
Devon TQ13 9NM
(01626) 835578
Visitors welcome, please telephone first

135
Ashley Howard *Fellow*
10 Pine Grove
Maidstone
Kent ME14 2AJ
(01622) 686390
Visitors by appointment please

136
Joanna Howells *Fellow*
30 School Street
Church Lawford
Rugby CV23 9EE
(01203) 544346
Visitors welcome by appointment

137
Anita Hoy *Honorary Fellow*
50 Julian Avenue
Acton
London W3 9JF
(0181) 992 4041
Visitors by appointment only

138
John Huggins *Fellow*
Ruardean Garden Pottery
Forest of Dean
Gloucestershire GL17 9TP
(01594) 543577
Fax: (01594) 544536
Workshop showroom open Monday – Saturday
9.00am-5.30pm. Summer Sundays 1-5pm

139
Edward Hughes
The Stables
Isel Hall
Cockermouth
Cumbria CA13 0QG
(01900) 825557
Visitors welcome by appointment

140
Simon Hulbert
Brook Street Pottery
Hay-on-Wye
Herefordshire HR3 5BQ
(01497) 821026
Fax: (01497) 821063

141
Bernard Irwin
The Barn
South Downs
Chyenhal
nr. Drift
Penzance
Cornwall TR19 6AW
Tel: (01736) 731899

142
Paul Jackson
Helland Bridge Pottery
Helland Bridge
Bodmin
Cornwall PL30 4QR
(01208) 75240
Visitors welcome, please telephone first

143
Anne James *Fellow*
Ashleigh
Gloucester Street
Painswick
Gloucestershire GL6 6QN
(01452) 81 3378
Visitors welcome, please telephone first

144
John Jelfs *Fellow*
The Pottery
Clapton Row
Bourton-on-the-Water
Gloucestershire GL54 2DN
(01451) 820173
Showroom open 9.00am-6.00pm Monday to
Saturday

145
Chris Jenkins *Fellow*
19 Towngate
Marsden
Huddersfield
Yorkshire HD7 6DD

(01484) 844444

Visitors welcome by appointment

146
Wendy Johnson *Fellow*
92 Nottingham Road
New Basford
Notts NG7 7AH

(0115) 9607940

Visitors welcome by appointment

147
Hazel Johnston *Fellow*
The Croft
North Street
Marton
Rugby
Warwickshire CV23 9RJ

(01926) 632467

Visitors welcome by appointment

148
Philip Jolley
44 Oakthorpe Road
Oxford OX2 7BE

(01865) 319276

Visitors welcome by appointment only

149
David Jones *Fellow*
Leamington Spa
Contact: c/o CPA
21 Carnaby Street
London W1V 1PH

150
Eileen Jones
Chapelgate Pottery
Chittlehamholt
nr. Umberleigh
Devon EX37 9NS

(01769) 540538

Open from 1 June to 30 September, 10.30am to 5pm daily except Wednesdays and Thursday. Other dates and times by appointment. Please telephone first

151
Vresh David Kanikanian
Gallery Tavid
56 St. Mary's Road
London W5 5EX

(0181) 566 1494

Visitors welcome, but please telephone first

152
Walter Keeler *Fellow*
Moorcroft Cottage
Penallt
Monmouth
Gwent NP5 4AH

Tel/Fax: (01600) 713 946

Visitors welcome but please telephone first

153
Julian King-Salter *Fellow*
Bancau
Brynberian
Crymych
Pembrokeshire SA41 3TS

(01239) 891652

Ring or write for showroom opening times, or to make an appointment

154
Gabriele Koch *Fellow*
147 Archway Road
London N6 5BL

(0181) 292 3169

Visitors welcome by appointment

155
Anna Lambert *Fellow*
Chapel Road
Steeton
W. Yorks BD20 6NU

(01535) 657003

Visitors welcome but please write or telephone first

156
Nigel Lambert *Fellow*
Golden Valley Cottage
Morse Lane
Drybrook
Gloucestershire
GL17 9BA

(01594) 542251

No showroom, but visitors welcome; please telephone first

157
Peter Lane *Fellow*
Ivy House
Jacklyns Lane
New Alresford
Hampshire SO24 9JU
(01962) 735041
Visitors welcome by appointment

158
Richard Launder *Fellow*
Ceramic Institute
National College of Art and Design
Stromgaten
Bergen 5015
Norway

159
David Leach OBE *Honorary Fellow*
Lowerdown Pottery
Bovey Tracey
Devon TQ13 9LE
(01626) 833408
Visitors are welcome at showroom 9am-6pm
weekdays, Saturdays 9am-1pm by appointment
only

160
Janet Leach *Honorary Fellow*
Leach Pottery
St Ives
Cornwall TR26 2HE
(01736) 796398
Showroom open 10am-5pm Mon.-Sat.

161
John Leach *Fellow*
Muchelney Pottery
nr Langport
Somerset TA10 0DW
(01458) 250324
Shop open (all year round) Monday-Friday 9am-
1pm, 2-5pm; Saturday 9am-1pm. Workshop
viewing by prior telephone appointment please.

162
Eileen Lewenstein *Honorary Fellow*
11 Western Esplanade
Portslade
Brighton
East Sussex BN41 1WE
(01273) 418705
Visitors welcome by appointment

163
Roger Lewis
6 Chellow Terrace
Bradford
West Yorks BD9 6AY
(01274) 495380
Visitors welcome by appointment

164
Gaynor Lindsell
Whalebones
Wood Street
Barnet
Herts. EN5 4BZ
Tel/Fax: (0181) 449 5288

165
Andy Lloyd
Oakhayes
Symonsbury
Bridport
Dorset DT6 3NR
(01308) 421931

166
Sophie MacCarthy
The Chocolate Factory
Farleigh Place
Hackney
London N16 7SX
(0171) 690 5091

167
Christine McCole
Hafod Hill Pottery
Llanboidy, Whitland
Carmarthenshire SA34 0ER
(01994) 448361
Visitors welcome

168
Laurence McGowan *Fellow*
6 Aughton
Collingbourne Kingston
Marlborough
Wilts SN8 3SA
(01264) 850 749
Visitors by appointment please

169
Lesley McShea
Unit 'E'
Spencer Mews
Spencer Avenue
Palmers Green
London N13
(0958) 473355 (Mobile)

170
Vinitha McWhinnie
22 Widney Manor Road
Solihull
West Midlands B91 3JQ
(0121) 705 8842
1/133 Custard Factory
Gibb Street
Digbeth
Birmingham B9 4AA
(0121) 604 7777 (messages)
Visitors welcome by appointment

171
Martin McWilliam
Auf dem Kötjen 1
26209 Sandhatten
Germany
Tel/Fax: (00 49) (0)4482 8372

172
Jane Maddison
The Old School Cottages
Stragglethorpe
Lincoln LN5 0GZ
(01400) 272971
Visitors welcome by appointment

173
Made in Cley
Cley next the Sea
Norfolk NR25 7RF
(01263) 740134
Gallery open all year

174
Mal Magson   *Fellow*
45 North Leas Avenue
Scarborough
YO12 6LJ
(01723) 362969
Enquries welcome, please write or phone

175
John Maguire
Strathearn Pottery
32 West High Street
Crieff
Perthshire PH7 4DL
(01764) 656100

176
Fenella Mallalieu   *Fellow*
100 Mortimer Road
London N1 4LA
(0171) 241 6553
Fax: (0171) 249 5341
Visitors by appointment

177
Jim Malone   *Fellow*
Hagget House
Towngate
Ainstable
Carlisle
Cumbria CA4 9RE
(01768) 896444
Showroom open daily from 9am onwards.
Visitors to workshop by appointment

178
Kate Malone   *Fellow*
157 Balls Pond Road
London N1 4BG
(0171) 254 4037
Fax (0171) 275 0401
(studio to rear on Culford Mews)

179
John Maltby   *Fellow*
The Orchard House
Stoneshill
Crediton
Devon EX17 4EF
(01363) 772753
Visitors welcome at any reasonable time. Please
telephone first

180
West Marshall   *Fellow*
118 White Hill
Chesham
Buckinghamshire
HP5 1AR
(01494) 785969
Very small workshop not suitable for visitors

181
Will Levi Marshall   *Fellow*
Orchardton Pottery
Auchencairn
Castle Douglas
Dumfries & Galloway
DG7 1QL, Scotland
(01556) 640399
Visitors by appointment only

182
John Mathieson
50 Ridgeway
Weston Favell
Northampton NN3 3AN
(01604) 409942
Visitors by appointment only please

183
Leo Francis Matthews   *Fellow*
Ivy Court
Shawbury
nr Shrewsbury
Shropshire SY4 4NL
(01903) 250 866
Visitors by appointment only

184
Marcio Mattos   *Fellow*
Farleigh Studios
The Chocolate Factory
Farleigh Place
London N16 7SX
(0171) 254 1351
Fax: (0171) 503 8417
Email: 106154.2636@compuserve.com
Visitors welcome but please ring first

185
Peter Meanley   *Fellow*
6 Downshire Road
Bangor
Co. Down
N. Ireland BT20 3TW
(01247) 466831
Visitors welcome, but please telephone first

186
Eric James Mellon   *Fellow*
5 Parkfield Avenue
Bognor Regis
West Sussex PO21 3BW
(01243) 268949
Clients by appointment

187
Kate Mellors
Rosemead
Marshwood
nr. Bridport
Dorset DT6 5QB
(01297) 678217
Visitors welcome but please telephone first

188
Nick Membery
Unit A6
8-9 Hoxton Square
London N1 6NU
(0171) 613 3538

189
Jon Middlemiss   *Fellow*
Wheal Vor Cottage
Tyringham Road
Leland, St Ives
Cornwall TR26 3LF
Tel/Fax: (01736) 754832
Visitors by appointment only

190
David Miller   *Fellow*
Rue du Ranc
30190 Collorgues
France
(00 33) (0) 4 66 81 91 19
and
33 St Andrew's Square
Surbiton
Surrey KT6 4EG
Visitors welcome; write or telephone first

191
Sean Miller
108 Dewsbury Road
London NW10 1EP
(0181) 208 0148

192
Toff Milway   *Fellow*
Conderton Pottery
The Old Forge
Conderton
nr. Tewkesbury
Glos. GL20 7PP
(01386) 725387

Workshop and showroom open Monday to
Saturday 9am-5.30pm. Phone at other times.
Always large selection of work on display

193
Jill Moger
The Studio
75 Millfield Lane
Nether Poppleton
York YO2 6NA

(01904) 794874

Studio visits by appointment

194
Ursula Mommens   *Honorary Fellow*
The Pottery
South Heighton
Newhaven
Sussex BN9 0HL

(01273) 514408

Open every day 9am-6pm

195
Sarah Monk
Eastnor Pottery
Clock Cottage
Home Farm
Eastnor
Ledbury
Herefordshire HR8 1RD

Tel/Fax: (01531) 633 255

Open every Sunday Easter until September. Other times by appointment

196
Tony James Moody
Silica City Studio
188 Bellingdon Road
Chesham
Bucks. HP5 2NN

(01494) 792438

197
Kim Morgan
Kalimna
Le Chemin du Portelet
La Route de Noirmont
St. Brelades
Jersey JE3 8AU

(01534) 490370

198
Aki Moriuchi   *Fellow*
1 Parkside Drive
Edgware
Middlesex HA8 8JU

Tel/Fax: (0181) 958 2639

Visitors by appointment only

199
Jenny Morten
31 Stanhope Road
Darlington
Co. Durham DL3 7AP

(01325) 463474

200
Roger Mulley
Clanfield Pottery
131 Chalton Lane
Clanfield
Waterlooville
Hampshire PO8 0RG

(01705) 595144

Visitors always welcome at weekends

201
John Mullin
September House
Parnacott
Holsworthy
Devon EX22 7JD

(01409) 253589

Studio open to the public. Visitors welcome

202
Sue Mundy
66 Highgrove Street
Reading RG1 5EN

(0118) 9872956

Visitors welcome but please telephone first

203
Stephen Murfitt
The Workshop
18 Stretham Road
Wicken
Cambs. CB7 5XH

(01353) 721160

Visitors welcome by appointment

204
Tessa Wolfe Murray
3rd Floor Studios
6 Carr Mills
322 Meanwood Road
Leeds LS7 2HY

(0113) 262 7704

Visitors welcome by appointment

205
Emily Myers   *Fellow*
c/o Working Wood
Crux Easton
Newbury
Berkshire RG20 9QF

Tel/Fax: (01635) 254435

Visitors by appointment only

206
Susan Nemeth   *Fellow*
Westland Studios
3rd Floor
3-11 Westland Place
London N1 7LP

(0171) 250 3224/249 0102

Visitors by appointment only

207
Christine Niblett
Sa Cantera
Calle Pastoritx 2
Son Vida
07013 Palma de Mallorca
Spain

(00 34) 71 791787

Only 10 minutes from centre of Palma. Visitors
welcome but best telephone first

208
Jacqueline Norris
Brocas Studios
81 High Street
Eton
Windsor
Berks. SL4 6AF

(01753) 860771
Fax: (01753) 622292
Email: etonarts@mail.bogo.co.uk

Visitors welcome to gallery at any time, studio
visits by appointment

209
Evelyn Papp
30 Derby Road
Bramcote
Nottingham NG9 3BA

(0115) 9254150

Visitors by appointment only

210
Stephen Parry
Ryburgh Pottery
Little Ryburgh
Fakenham
Norfolk NR21 0LP

(01328) 829543

Visitors welcome. Advisable to telephone if
making a special journey

211
Colin Pearson   *Honorary Fellow*
3 Mountfort Terrace
Barnsbury Square
London N1 1JJ

Tel/Fax: (0171) 607 1965
Studio and Gallery
15-17 Cloudesley Road
London N1 0EL

(0958) 387744 (Mobile)

The studio and gallery are a short walk from the
Angel, Islington, or the Crafts Council Gallery,
Pentonville Road. Transport by Underground:
Angel. By bus: 73, 19, 38, 171 or 4. Cars should
approach via Copenhagen Street. Visitors to the
gallery are welcome, but telephone first

212
Katrina Pechal
57 Thornhill Road
Surbiton
Surrey KT6 7TJ

(0181) 390 9205

213
Carol Peevor
76 Park Lane
Wednesbury
West Midlands WS10 9PT

(0121) 556 0247

Visitors (occasional) by appointment please

214
Jane Perryman   *Fellow*
Wash Cottage
Clare Road
Hunden
Suffolk CO10 8DH

Tel/Fax: (01440) 786228

Visitors are welcome by appointment only

215
Richard Phethean   *Fellow*
76 Oglander Road
London SE15 4EN
(0171) 639 1521
Visitors welcome by arrangement

216
Nancy Pickard
55 Kings Road
Canton
Cardiff
CF1 9DA
(01222) 373424
Visitors welcome by appointment. Information
pack on request

217
Ian Pirie   *Fellow*
8 St Michael's Place
Newton Hill
Stonehaven
Kincardineshire
(01569) 730908

218
John Pollex   *Fellow*
White Lane Gallery
1 White Lane
Barbican
Plymouth
Devon PL1 2LP
(01752) 662338/224902
Email: pollex@mail.zynet.co.uk
Gallery open throughout the year 10am-5pm.
Visitors to the workshop by appointment

219
Philomena Pretsell
Rose Cottage
10 Fountain Place
Loanhead
Midlothian EH20 9EA
(0131) 440 0751
Workshop at home, 5 miles from Edinburgh,
with visitors welcome by appointment

220
Ursula Morley Price
Chez Gaty
Vaux Lavalette
16320 Villebois Lavalette
France
(00 33) 545259167

221
Paul Priest
71 Sunnycroft
Downley
High Wycombe
Bucks HP13 5UR
(01494) 465715

222
Nick Rees
Muchelney Pottery
Langport
Somerset TA10 6DW
(01458) 250324

223
Gaynor Reeve
Callis Court
London Road
West Malling
Kent ME19 5AH
(01732) 872469

224
Peter Reynolds
Balaclava Pottery
The Street
Lyng
Norfolk NR9 5QZ
(01603) 872191
Visitors welcome by appointment

225
Mary Rich   *Fellow*
Penwerris Pottery
Cowlands Creek
Old Kea
nr Truro
Cornwall TR3 6AT
Tel/Fax: (01872) 276926
There is no showroom, but visitors are welcome
by prior appointment

226
Christine-Ann Richards   *Fellow*
Chapel House
High Street
Wanstrow
nr. Shepton Mallet
Somerset BA4 4TB
(01749) 850 208
Visitors to the workshop by appointment only

227
Audrey Richardson
Morawel
Parrog Road
Newport
Pembrokeshire SA42 0RF

(01239) 820 449

Visitors welcome by appointment

228
David Roberts   *Fellow*
Cressfield House
44 Upperthong Lane
Holmfirth
Huddersfield
West Yorkshire HD7 1BQ

Tel/Fax: (01484) 685110

No showroom but visitors are welcome to
workshop by appointment

229
Hilary Roberts
410 Haven Mews
St Pauls Way
London E3 4AG

(0181) 983 1323

230
Jim Robison   *Fellow*
Booth House Gallery
3 Booth House
Holmfirth
Huddersfield
W. Yorkshire HD7 1QA

(01484) 685270

Studio and Gallery open to the public at
weekends and by appointment

231
Phil Rogers   *Fellow*
Marston Pottery
Lower Cefn Faes
Rhayader
Powys LD6 5LT

Tel/Fax: (01597) 810875

Showroom half-mile from Rhayader centre.
Signposted from car park. Visitors welcome at
showroom at any reasonable time and to the
workshop by appointment. Please telephone first
if coming a long distance particularly in the
winter months.

232
Margaret Rollason
19 Oakside Close
Evington
Leicester LE5 6SN

(0116) 2412188

Visitors welcome, please telephone first

233
Duncan Ross   *Fellow*
Daneshay House
71 Alma Lane
Hale
Farnham
Surrey GU9 0LT

(01252) 710704

Visitors to showroom welcome; please telephone

234
Elizabeth Roussel
26 High Street
Woodstock
Oxfordshire OX20 1TG

(01993) 811298

Visitors welcome by appointment

235
Antonia Salmon   *Fellow*
20 Adelaide Road
Nether Edge
Sheffield S7 1SQ

(0114) 2585971

Visitors welcome by appointment only

236
Robert Sanderson
Cowden Cottage
Abercairny
Crieff
Perthshire PH7 3QZ

(01764) 683273

237
Patrick Sargent   *Fellow*
Glaserberg
3453 Heimisbach
Switzerland

(00 41) 34 4312244

Visitors welcome by prior arrangement. Students
and ex students with genuine interest in firing
with wood are often accepted for working
periods

238
Nicolette Savage
145 Goodhart Way
West Wickham
Kent BR4 0EU

(0181) 777 8372

239
Micki Schloessingk   *Fellow*
Bridge Pottery
Cheriton
Gower
Swansea SA3 1BY

(01792) 386279

Visitors are welcome but please telephone first

240
David Scott   *Fellow*
33 Cross Lane
Mountsorrel
Leics. LE12 7BU

(0116) 2302100

Visitors welcome by appointment

241
Wim Seelde
6 Bute Street
Brighton
East Sussex BN2 2EH

(01273) 626116

242
Sheila Seepersaud-Jones
Studio 'M'
5 Brookland Rise
London NW11 6DN

(0181) 458 5530

243
Sarah Jane Selwood   *Fellow*
15 North Fort Street
Edinburgh EH6 4HB

(0131) 555 6075

244
Ken and Valerie Shelton
Shelton Pottery
18 Heath End Road
Alsager
Stoke-on-Trent ST7 2SQ

(01270) 872686

245
Ray Silverman   *Fellow*
35 Dunster Crescent
Hornchurch
Essex RM11 3QD

(01708) 458864

Visitors by appointment

246
Penny Simpson
44a Court Street
Moretonhampstead
Devon TQ13 8LG

Tel/Fax: (01647) 440708

Workshop and Showroom open to visitors,
Monday-Friday 9.30am-5pm and some
weekends. Telephone first if making special
journey

247
Graham Skinner
Studio One
1 Victoria Street
Rochester
Kent ME1 1XJ

(01634) 811469

Visitors welcome by appointment

248
Michael Skipwith   *Fellow*
Lotus Pottery
Stoke Gabriel
Totnes
S. Devon TQ9 6SL

(01803) 782 303

Workshop and showroom open Monday to Friday
9am-12.30 and 2pm-5.30pm. Saturdays by
appointment

249
Richard Slee   *Fellow*
12A Upper Hamilton Road
Brighton
East Sussex BN1 5DF

250
Daniel Smith
Archway Ceramics
410 Haven Mews
23 St Paul's Way
London E3 4AG

(0181) 983 1323

251
Keith Smith
Otterton Mill Pottery
Otterton
Devon

(01395) 567041
(01297) 552404 (Home)

Restaurant, shop and other workshops on site,
free parking. I try to be open 10.30-5pm every
day from Easter to October, but a phone call will
make sure

252
Mark Smith
11 School Lane
Sudbury
Ashbourne
Derbyshire DE6 5HZ

(01283) 585219

Visitors by appointment

253
Peter Smith   *Fellow*
Higher Bojewyan
Pendeen
Penzance
Cornwall TR19 7TR

(01736) 788820

Visitors welcome

254
John Solly   *Fellow*
Goldspur Cottage
Flackley Ash
Peasmarsh
Rye
East Sussex TN31 6YH

(01797) 230 276

The pottery is opposite the Flackley Ash Hotel on
the A268. Visitors are welcome at any time, but if
coming from afar, please telephone first

255
Charles Spacey
Studio Ceramics
Pant-y-Ddafad
Pont Robert
Meifod
Powys SY22 6JF

(01938) 500 620

Visitors welcome but please telephone first

256
Chris Speyer   *Fellow*
Yerja Ceramics & Textiles
Mill Rise
Ford Road
Bampton
Devon EX16 9LW

Tel/Fax: (01398) 331163

Visitors welcome but telephone first

257
Rupert Spira
Church Farm
More
Bishop's Castle
Shropshire SY9 5HH

Tel/Fax: (01588) 650 588

258
Christel Spriet
7 Green Man Lane
Harston
Cambridge CB2 5PY

(01223) 872 761

Studio open by appointment

259
Peter Stoodley   *Fellow*
Little Rings
Buckland Rings
Sway Road
Lymington
Hampshire SO41 8NN

(01590) 679778

Visitors welcome by appointment

260
Harry Horlock Stringer   *Fellow*
Taggs Yard School of Ceramics
23 Woodlands Road
Barnes
London SW13 0JZ

Tel/Fax: (0181) 876 5750

Visits arranged by telephone appointments only

261
Helen Swain   *Fellow*
8 Fyfield Road
Waltham Forest
London E17 3RG

(0181) 520 4043

This is a one-person pottery, so visitors by
appointment and, sorry, no students possible

262
TAJA
Pottery House
38 Cross Street
Moretonhampstead
Devon TQ13 8NL
(01647) 440782

263
Rebecca Taylor
18 Clarion House
St. Anne's Court
Soho
London W1V 3AX
(0171) 434 2924

264
Sutton Taylor   *Fellow*
c/o Hart Gallery
23 Main Street
Linby
Nottingham NG15 8AE
(0115) 963 8707
Fax: (0115) 964 0743

265
Sabina Teuteberg   *Fellow*
86 Cecilia Road
London E8 2ET
(0171) 241 5279
Visitors welcome, but by appointment only

266
Lyndon Thomas
Swn y Mor
Llanarth
Aberaeron
Dyfed SA47 0PZ
(01545) 580406
Visitors welcome by appointment

267
Owen Thorpe   *Fellow*
Churchstoke Pottery
Old School
Castle Street
Churchstoke
Powys SY15 6AG
(01588) 620 511
(01938) 561 618
Open 9.30am – 2.00pm. Other times by
appointment

268
Anna Timlett
3 Mill Cottages
Coldharbour Mill
Uffculme
Cullompton
Devon EX15 3EE
(01884) 841315

269
Mark de la Torre
The Courtyard Flat
The Old Rectory
Stoke Lacy
Hereford HR7 4HH

270
Marianne de Trey   *Honorary Fellow*
The Cabin
Shinners Bridge
Dartington, Totnes
Devon TQ9 6JB
(01803) 862046 (after 6pm)
Visitors preferably by appointment

271
Judy Trim   *Fellow*
3 Coningham Mews
London W12 9QW
(0181) 749 1190
Fax: (0181) 749 1190
Visitors by appointment

272
Katrina Trinick
Lesquite
Lanivet
Bodmin
Cornwall PL30 5HT
(01208) 831716
Visitors welcome but please telephone first

273
Fran Tristram
42 Seymour Road
West Bridgford
Nottingham NG2 5EP
(0115) 9822681

274
Ruthanne Tudball   *Fellow*
Norfolk House
344 Wokingham Road
Earley, Reading
Berks. RG6 7DE

(01734) 268003
From Jan.1998: (0118) 9268003

I have no showroom but visitors are welcome to
the workshop by appointment only

275
Tydd Pottery
Pode Hole
Spalding
Lincs. PE11 3QA

(01775) 766120

276
Sue Varley
54 Elthorne Road
Uxbridge
Middlesex UB8 2PS

(01895) 231738
Fax: (01895) 813907

Visitors welcome but please telephone first

277
Tina Vlassopulos   *Fellow*
29 Canfield Gardens
London NW6 3JP
(0171) 624 4582

Fax: (0171) 328 1483

Visitors by appointment

278
Edmund de Waal   *Fellow*
9 Maude Road
Camberwell
London SE5 8NY

(0171) 703 5867
Fax: (0171) 701 5079

279
Carol Wainwright
Little Durnford
Old Malthouse Lane
Langton Matravers
Dorset BH19 3HH

(01929) 425905

Visitors by appointment

280
Josie Walter   *Fellow*
The Pottery
22 Nan Gells Hill
Bolehill
Derbyshire DE4 4GN

Tel/Fax: 01629 823669
Email: 106137.713@compuserve.com

Visitors always welcome. Please telephone to
check we are here

281
Sarah Walton   *Fellow*
Keeper's Cottage
Selmeston
nr. Polegate
Sussex BN62 6UH

(01323) 811284/811517

282
John Ward   *Fellow*
Fachongle Uchaf
Cilgwyn
Newport
Dyfed SA42 0QR

(01239) 820 706

Visitors by appointment

283
Sasha Wardell   *Fellow*
36 Tory
Bradford-on-Avon
Wiltshire BA15 1NN

(01225) 868756

Visitors by prior arrangement

284
Andrew Watts
Lannock Pottery
Weston
Hitchin
Herts. SG4 7EE

Tel/Fax: (01462) 790356

Visitors welcome during normal working hours,
but by appointment only at weekends

285
Nicola Werner
The Old Parsonage
Hemyock
nr. Cullompton
Devon EX15 3RG

(01823) 680957

Visitors welcome but by appointment only

286
Gilda Westermann
Archway Ceramics
410 Haven Mews
St. Paul's Way
London E3 4AQ
(0181) 983 1323

287
John Wheeldon   *Fellow*
West End Gallery
4 West End
Wirksworth
Derbyshire DE4 4EG
(01629) 822356
Fax: (01629) 826545
Showroom open 10.30-5.30 Thursday-Sat. Also
by appointment

288
Rob Whelpton
54a Victoria Road
Warminster
Wiltshire BA12 8HF
(01985) 219577
Visitors to workshop welcome but please ring
first

289
David White   *Fellow*
4 Callis Court Road
Broadstairs
Kent CT10 3AE
(01843) 863145
No showroom, but please telephone

290
David Constantine White
Briar Hey Pottery
Burnley Road
Mytholmroyd
West Yorkshire HX7 5PG
(01422) 885725
Open usual trading hours

291
Mary White   *Fellow*
Zimmerplatzweg 6
55599 Wonsheim
Germany
(00 49) 0 6703/2922
Visitors welcome, but please telephone first

292
Tony White
Upper Lodge
Hafod
Cwmystwyth
Ysrad Meurig
Ceredigion SY25 6DX
Wales
(01974) 282202

293
Caroline Whyman   *Fellow*
21 Iliffe Yard
Crampton Street
London SE17 3QA
Tel/Fax: (0171) 708 5904
Visitors are requested to phone or fax for an
appointment

294
Maggie Williams
Poulders
65 Ospringe Street
Ospringe
Faversham
Kent ME13 8TW
(01795) 531768

295
Peter Wills
44 Newcastle Hill
Bridgend
Mid Glamorgan CF31 4EY
(01656) 662902

296
George Wilson
48B Mulgrave Road
Ealing
London W5 1LE
(0181) 998 4470
Visitors welcome by appointment

297
David Winkley   *Fellow*
Vellow Pottery
Lower Vellow
Williton
Taunton
Somerset TA4 4LS
(01984) 656458
Workshop and pottery open to visitors from
8.30am until 6pm Monday to Saturday

298
Mary Wondrausch *Fellow*
The Pottery
Brickfields
Compton
nr Guildford
Surrey GU3 1HZ

(01483) 414097

Mon-Fri. 9am-5pm; Saturday and Sunday 2-5pm

299
Gary Wood *Fellow*
Dryleaze
Box Road, Bathford
Bath BA1 7LR

Tel/Fax: (01225) 858888

300
Karen Ann Wood *Fellow*
3 Foxgrove Avenue
Beckenham
Kent BR3 5BA

(0181) 658 2759

Visitors welcome but should telephone
beforehand

301
Steve Woodhead *Fellow*
65 Shakespeare Gardens
Rugby
Warwickshire CV22 6HA

(01788) 522178

Visitors welcome, but please telephone first

302
Rosemary D Wren ARCA *Honorary Fellow*
and Peter M Crotty
The Oxshott Pottery
Nutwood Steading
Strathpeffer
Ross-shire IV14 9DT
Scotland

(01997) 421 478

Visitors are welcome but please telephone first.
Strathpeffer – a Victorian spa – is on the central
Highland east-west road A834, 20 miles NW of
Inverness. Take the M9/A9 from Stirling and turn
off through Dingwall (thus avoiding Strathpeffer
by-pass). The Nutwood drive is on the right just
before the 30 mph sign. From London by road is
571 miles; 13 hours by train; 1½ hours by air
Heathrow/Inverness

303
Gill Wright
52 South Street
Epsom
Surrey KT18 7PQ

(01372) 723908

Visitors very welcome but please telephone for
appointment first

304
Muriel P Wright *Fellow*
Ashanwell
Potkins Lane
Orford, Woodbridge
Suffolk IP12 2SS

(01394) 450580

Oxidised stoneware, glazed white with blue
decoration. Lamps, bowls, dishes and fountain
bowls. Trained at Manchester College of Art.
Potting for over 30 years. Founder member of
CPA. Visitors welcome but telephone call essential

305
Takeshi Yasuda *Fellow*
37 Kensington Gardens
Bath BA1 6LH

Tel: (01225) 334136
Fax: (01225) 313492

Visitors welcome but by appointment only

306
Joanna and Andrew Young *Fellows*
A & J Young Pottery
Common Farm
Sustead Road
Lower Gresham
Norfolk NR11 8RE

(01263) 577 548

Small shop open at Common Farm every
weekday. For weekend opening times and
directions please telephone

WORKING WITH CLAY

The opportunities for studying ceramics are many and varied depending on the sort of committment you are able to make. Courses range from full-time and part-time in art departments in colleges of further education and universities, to part-time courses at local institutes and weekends with well-known potters. There are now a plethora of books and videos so you can teaching yourself. Here the various possibilities are detailed under different headings.

Short Courses

Many well-established potters offer short courses aimed either at the beginner or the more experienced maker. These may be for one day to two weeks or more. Many of these courses are listed in each issue of of *Ceramic Review* and most will supply a brochure outlining what is offered. It is often useful to ask to speak to people who have been on the course if you want a user's view and to obtain as much information about the facilities available so you are not disappointed. For many with a full-time job, such courses serve as an enjoyable and rewarding working holiday.

Videos and Films

Many videos and films of potters at work are available. They serve as a good guide to the working methods of individual potters, though they are no real substitute for an experienced teacher who can answer questions and deal with your particular need. However, they are excellent as back-up material. A free list of available videos and films on craft and design (including ceramics) can be obtained from the Crafts Council, 44a Pentonville Road, London N1 9BY, and new videos on the market are reviewed in *Ceramic Review*.

Part-time Courses

In addition to full-time courses many BA (Hons) courses are now open to part-time students who spread the degree over 5 or 6 years. In addition local education authorities offer a wide range of part-time courses. Some are classed as 'Non-vocational' but many have been set up to give a first-class education so that, over a period of time, they provide a thorough training in studio pottery techniques. Many Art Colleges, Technical Colleges and Colleges of Adult and Further Education (including some of the ones listed here) offer such courses, some giving their own certificate of proficiency. As the intake is irregular and the age and standard of students variable it is usual for each student to follow his/her own course of indefinite duration. Particulars of these and evening institutes in the area can be obtained from your local Adult Education Centre or from the Chief Education Officer of your Education Authority.

Local education authorities also provide evening and day part-time courses for beginners and for more advanced students. Classes last approximately two hours. Fees are relatively modest and concessions may be offered for people out of work. Basic materials are usually provided and finished work can be purchased at a minimal cost. Personal tools are not usually supplied. Instructors vary in skill and teaching ability and it is worth asking other students how they have fared. Full information on available classes can be obtained from your local Public Library or Education Office. In London the booklet *Floodlight* lists all currently available classes and can be obtained through most newsagents and bookshops. New sessions start in September each year. It is worth remembering that pottery classes are usually very popular so book early. However, some vacant places occur during the year which can be taken up by new students.

Workshop Training

Because of the very diverse nature of studio pottery few formal apprenticeship schemes exist for training prospective potters at present, though with the introduction of National Vocational Qualifications (NVQs) by the government some nationally recognised basis will be set up. The kind of work undertaken by trainees, and the amount and quality of the teaching they receive in the studio of the individual potter will depend largely on the skill and outlook of the potter they work for, and the agreement that is made. While few potters will, or are able to, offer a full-time, two-year training, many will take an assistant for a few days or weeks for specific projects.

Joining a workshop requires determination and a degree of luck. The number of potters employing assistants is small, demand for places often exceeds supply, and competition is, therefore, fierce. Success in finding a potter to work with whose pots you admire will require commitment, strong perseverance and almost certainly some measure of being in the right place at the right time.

You can try to join a pottery direct as a trainee assistant with little or no previous experience, or for a period of workshop practice following an art school ceramics course. One with a strong bias towards studio pottery would be an advantage.

The work of some potters is so individual that it almost precludes additional help. Those who do employ assistants often spend much of their time making repetition ware, decorative or functional. Students leaving art schools for workshops may find the change constricting and it is best to bear this in mind. Much of the learning will inevitably be done by making pots designed initially by the potters and the opportunities for personal expression are likely to be limited.

There are no standard rates of pay for trainees and remuneration will be set according to their means in relation to the real productive help that an assistant can give. It is the experience of many potters that assistants often over-estimate their ability to make pots quickly and of a saleable quality. Some potters regard the training as payment. The Crafts Council offer a variety of Training Grant Schemes. Some are intended for established craftworkers and these are a great help in supplementing the wages of trainees. But this scheme is not automatically available to every potter with assistants and it must be assumed that the rate of pay for trainees will be less - and in some cases considerably less - than those in industry or teaching.

All the names and addresses of Fellows and Professional Members of the Craft Potters Association are listed in this book. Trainee positions are often advertised in *Ceramic Review* and many other potters are included in *Visiting Craft Workshops* published by the Rural Development Commission. A list of potters who work with assistants can be obtained from the Crafts Council. Regional Art Boards usually have a Craft Officer who can give useful advice on opportunities available within the area covered by each Board.

Application to Studios

Before applying to work with a potter try to see the work of as many potters as you can so that you are clear about the kind of pots you want to make. If, for example, your main interest is ceramic sculpture you are likely to be happier working with a potter whose prime interest this is, than one preoccupied with domestic ware. Just writing a letter which says, in essence, 'I am interested in pottery. Do you have a job?' is unlikely to gain a positive response. Potters get many such letters from applicants who appear to post a dozen or so at a time to widely differing potters in the hope that something will turn up.

The better, and probably only, way is to go and see the potters of your choice in their studios. This requires a great deal of effort, it is time-consuming and demands perseverance mentioned earlier. But in seeking a workshop place you are, in effect, asking potters to make a commitment to you in time, energy and money. Potters have livings to earn and they must be as sure as they can that you are really serious about working with them to mutual advantage. In short they have to be convinced that there is something in it for them as well as you.

Before you visit, telephone or write to see that it is convenient. Take with you any examples or photographs of pots you have made. Without some evidence it is very difficult for potters to judge an applicant's ability or potential.

Working successfully and harmoniously as a member of a small team, or in conjunction with an individual potter, is as much a question of good personal relationships as the teaching and acquisition of skills. In the search for workshop places, therefore, it is difficult to over-estimate the value of personal contact. This works both ways: it enables potters to judge at first hand an applicant's response to the work they do and, equally important, it gives applicants the opportunity to see what facilities are available and to say what they can offer the workshop. Trainees have much to give in enthusiasm for and commitment to working with clay, and in ready willingness to share all the many and sometimes tedious jobs that every workshop has to undertake to produce finished pots.

Setting up your own workshop

Once you have aquired sufficient knowledge and experience in pottery, whether by formal eductation or a mixture of evening classes and teaching yourself, you may wish to find a space in which to do your work. In many areas there are increasing opportunities to rent space in group workshops. This has the advantage of spreading the cost of overheads such as lighting and heating and it is often possible to share equipment with fellow makers. Many also relish the company and encouragement of others while they work.

You may be setting up a workshop for pleasure, for part-time self-employment or full-time potting. The requirements will depend on your particular needs as a potter; your type of kiln (gas, electric, wood-fired etc.), your method of production, and whether you will be open to the public for direct sales, to name but a few. As with any venture which requires the outlay of capital it is vital that you thoroughly research your requirements and the viability of your work to cover your costs. Help is freely on hand from many business advice organisations. They can assist with putting together a business plan - something which most colleges do not cover, but which will be essential for planning finances, especially if you intend to be self employed.

Details of organisations set up to help small crafts business can be obtained from the Crafts Council, 44a Pentonville Road, London N1 9BY. The Council also publish a book Running a Workshop which covers all the essentials, and has an extensive section covering sources of information advice, and grants. The monthly magazine Artist's Newsletter is another source of up to date information, and carries advertisements for studio space to hire. The classified section of Ceramic Review is a good starting point for second hand equipment. Equally useful is the Crafts Council publication Functional Pottery in Britain, which gives a brief history of studio pottery in the UK, with information on workshops, grants, exhibitions and such like.

Courses in art colleges, colleges of further education and universities

Graduate level courses BA (Hons)

These three or four year Courses (full-time) preceded by a one or two year Foundation Course aim for the development of the individual rather than his/her training for a specific employment situation. Entry is highly competitive and educational requirements stringent (usually 5 GCSEs passes although some colleges demand one or two 'A' level passes). Pottery (Ceramics) is usually contained in three dimensional design, and courses may include work in other media as well as Art History and Complementary Studies. In the Colleges offering Ceramics as a chief study the emphasis varies between craft, fine-art and industrial design pottery. Intending students should study prospectuses or visit courses before making application. End of year degree shows also provide an opportunity to talk to graduating students; many colleges now take part in the *New Designers* show each summer at the Business Design Centre in Islington, London.

For residents in the UK grants for these courses are mandatory, once a place has been secured, but are subject to means tests and other certain conditions. Overseas students usually have to pay full fees.

Vocational courses and BTEC

These courses differ from the above in these respects

- Entry requirements are usually less stringent.
- Courses are geared more towards professional training for subsequent employment as a technician, craftworker, designer/craftworker or designer.
- Grants are at the discretion of the LEAs.
- Courses vary from 1– 4 years.
- Courses, which usually lead to a local, regional or professional Diploma or Licentiateship include some ancillary studies in drawing, design and other craft techniques.

No official 'sandwich' courses for studio potters exist at present but some colleges make informal arrangements for students to work in potters' workshops during the course or in vacations

Colleges offering courses in ceramics

College	Course, entry requirements & qualifications and description of course supplied by college
ENGLAND **Alsager** **Crewe & Alsager Faculty** The Manchester Metropolitan University Hassall Road Alsager Staffs. ST7 2HL Tel: (0161) 247 5302 Fax: (0161) 247 6377	**BA (Hons) Crafts** Combined Studies: Wood/Metal/Ceramics/Textiles. Course description: The course gives a grounding in each of the four materials during the first half-year, after which students select two for continuing combined exploration. This encourages unusual and inventive approaches to media and techniques. Visual and historical research are integral, complementary elements of the degree. Also included in the course are a dissertation and a Business Unit dealing with both basic skills and a small business planning project.
Amersham **Amersham & Wycombe College** Stanley Hill Amersham Bucks HP7 9HN Tel: (01494) 735555 Fax: (01494) 735566	Ceramics included as an element in our Art College Foundation course, **BTEC General Art & Design course** 'A' Level Ceramics – entry GCSE in Art or Ceramics together with portfolio of art and design Evening classes in Pottery These courses act as feeders to courses of higher education namely HND or B.A. in Ceramics or associate subjects. Part-time courses (11 weeks) starting January, April and September.
Bath **Bath College of Higher Education** Faculty of Art and music Sion Hill Place Lansdown Bath BA1 5SF Tel: (01225) 425254 Fax: (01225) 445228	**BA (Hons) Ceramics** The course is designed to equip students with an understanding of contemporary ceramics and an education in the broad range of approaches, techniques, craft skills and industrial processes. Supporting studies offer options to work in other mediums and Complementary Studies develop analytical and critical skills, placing Art and Design activities amongst the other cultural, historical and social practices.
Birmingham **Birmingham Institute of Art and Design** University of Central England Corporation Street Birmingham B4 7DX Tel: (0121) 331 5819/5820	**BA (Hons) Three Dimensional Design Ceramics with Glass** 1 year foundation course or equivalent UCAS entry. Wide range of design content – architectural ceramics/glass: giftware, tableware, tiles, horticultural ware, lighting design, studio pottery. Materials and design-linked projects within 3DD course plus choice of electives in Fine Art, Fashion and Textiles, Jewellery and Visual Communication.

Bradford	**Bradford & Ilkley Community College** School of Art, Design & Textiles Great Horton Road Bradford West Yorkshire BD7 1AY Tel: (01274) 753239	**NCFE in Art & Design Access Studies.** A specialist Ceramic option available at Level 2 allowing students to progress to further special study at F. E. Bradford & H. E. Levels. **BTEC GNVQ Advanced Art & Design.** Broad Art & Design experience including Ceramics moving towards specialist Ceramic experience as the course progresses. Appropriate for students who wish to progress to H.E. in a 3D/Ceramic specialism. **BA (Hons) Art & Design.** A course which allows students to interrelate media areas across Art and/or Design. Students may combine Ceramics with one of the following: Painting, Illustration, Graphics, Textiles or Printmaking.
Brighton	**University of Brighton** Faculty of Art Design and Humanities Grand Parade Brighton BN2 2JY Tel: (01273) 643081 Fax: (01273) 643055	**BA (Hons) Three Dimensional Crafts** Wood, Metal, Ceramics, Plastics and Visual Research. This course offers specialisms in studio materials and visual research for the Artist-Craftsperson and Designer-Maker. Its students enjoy exploring processes and techniques towards the making of artifacts – whether, expressive, Decorative or functional. 3 years full-time. **BA (Hons) Three Dimensional Design for Production.** This course, having a shared diagnostic first year with Three Dimensional Crafts, has a strong involvement in materials, workshop practice and visual research. It offers the designer a combination of materials-based workshop skills, conceptual and developmental procedures and contextural research through a variety of project types suitable for small-scale production and interdisciplinary design. 3 years full-time.
Bristol	**UWE Bristol** Faculty of Art, Media & Design Clanage Road, Bower Ashton Bristol BS3 2J Tel: (0117) 9660222 x 475	**BA (Hons) Ceramics.** The course provides a broad experience of ceramics. Established techniques are studied forming the basis for independent development. Students can take advantage of the faculty-wide modular scheme which offers an extensive range of practical and theoretical art and design studies.Modules are designed to stimulate interest not only in the intrinsic and expressive qualities of ceramics but also in the exciting areas where complementary disciplines overlap. The final year centres on individual, self-directed, programmes of work.

| Canterbury | **Christchurch Canterbury College**
North Holmes Road
Canterbury
Kent CT1 1QU
Tel: (01227) 767700
Fax: (01227) 470442 | **B.A.Hons Ceramics or Art & Design.** Ceramics is offered as a single subject or combined with Painting, Printmaking or Sculpture.
B.A. Joint Hons. Ceramics is offered combined with any one of 16 other subjects e.g. Applied Social Science, English, Business Studies, American Studies, Music, etc.
These courses embrace both the functional and sculptural possibilities of clay and ceramic processes. They offer a comprehensive and challenging programme in both theory and practice in a stimulating and friendly environment.
M.A. Ceramics (2 years part-time. 1 year full-time) Offered as a taught course aimed at practising artists/ceramists with their own studio within travelling distance of the college. Taught in conjunction with painters, printmakers and sculptors. |
| Carlisle | **Cumbria College of Art & Design**
Brampton Road
Carlisle
Cumbria CA3 9AY
Tel: (01228) 25333
Fax: (01228) 514491 | **BA (Hons) Design Crafts** This is a multi-disciplinary course providing students with the opportunity to study ceramics with multi-media textiles, printed textiles, wood and metal. Students initially undertake all craft options in the first year, prior to specialising in their chosen craft area during the second and third year of the course. The practical craft options are supported by modules in Visual Research and Design Development, Business Awareness, Cultural Studies and Design History. The course can be studied either on a full or part-time basis.
H.N.D.BTEC in Design Crafts Students have the opportunity to study ceramics with a range of complementary craft options including Multimedia Textiles, Printed Textiles, Wood and Metal. Towards the end of the first year students begin to specialize in their chosen craft area, leading to a range of second year projects aimed at producing well-designed high quality craftwork. The craft options are supported by modules in Visual Studies, Design Development, Business and Professional Practice and Craft Management. |

Derby	**University of Derby** Britannia Mill Mackworth Road Derby DE22 3BL Tel: (01332) 622216 Email: V.Pickard@derby.ac.uk	**BA Hons Applied Arts.** Applied Arts is exceptionally well resourced with extensive ceramic, jewellery, fine/structural metal, glass and wood workshops. The course offers students the opportunity to experiment with a range of Applied Arts disciplines as well as specialise in ceramics. Students benefit from innovative, diverse and traditional approaches to processes and materials and are encouraged to use the courses multi-disciplinary character to inform their ceramic development. The course is ideal for students who are interested in making and enthusiastic to anticipate the future nature of Applied Arts practice. Entry requirements for students under 21 are normally 2 'A' levels and 5 GCSEs at C or above; if over 21 no formal qualifications may be necessary.
Eastbourne	**Eastbourne College of Arts & Technology** Eversley Court St. Anne's Road Eastbourne Sussex BN21 2HS Tel: (01323) 644711 Fax: (01323) 735090	**One-year BTEC Art Foundation. 2-year BTEC General Art & Design.** Ceramics specialist design option. City and Guilds 2-year part-time and OCN3 1-year part-time Advanced Ceramics Diploma in Creative Ceramic Studies.
Exeter	**Exeter School of Art and Design** University of Plymouth Earl Richards Road North Exeter EX2 6AS Tel: (01392) 475022	**BA (Hons) 3 Dimensional Design** **BA (Hons) Fine Art**
Falmouth	**Falmouth College of Arts** Woodlane Falmouth Cornwall TR11 4RA Tel: (01326) 211077 Fax: (01326) 319583	**BA (Hons) Studio Ceramics.** This programme aims to develop each student's individual interests and aspirations through the medium of studio ceramics. Central to this is the creation of a supportive environment which encourages and develops an independent approach to learning. This is not only built on a broad range of knowledge of technique, process and the associated technology, but also through an understanding of core values of learning from each other, communicating, researching, being open to new ideas and understanding the role of independent critical evaluation within an historical and cultural context. Students prepares for their own vision of the future.

Farnham	**The Surrey Institute of Art and Design** Falkner Road Farnham Surrey GU9 7DS Tel: (01252) 722441 Fax: (01252) 733869	**BA (Hons) 3DD Ceramics.** 5 GCSEs Grade C or above. Applicants normally will have successfully completed a Foundation Course or BTEC National Diploma. Ceramics is part of the BA (Hons) Three Dimensional Design which has a modular structure and embraces three specialist material areas Ceramics, Glass and Metals in the Faculty of Design. The programme offers a stimulating and challenging opportunity to study in exceptionally well - equipped studios. The Institute also has Full-time and Part-time MA courses.
Gloucester	**Royal Forest of Dean College** Five Acres Campus Coleford Gloucestershire GL16 7JT Tel: (01594) 833416 Fax: (01594) 837497	**BTEC National Diploma in Studio Ceramics** A two-year studio ceramics course aimed at students wishing to set up their own workshops or progress to Degree level courses. Students specialise after an introductory programme including a range of production techniques, glazing, kiln building and firing. Supporting studies include drawing, design and a range of visiting practitioners. Modern .purpose-built studios. Applications from mature students welcome. Advisory interviews may be made by telephone.
Harrogate	**Harrogate College** Hornbeam Park Hookstone Road Harrogate North Yorkshire HG2 8QT Tel: (01423) 879466 (01423) 878231	**Variety of Courses** to suit full-time, part-time, specialist and combined study in Ceramics, including BTEC National Diploma, HNC, City and Guilds and GNVQ. The facilities are excellent, with every opportunity for all aspects of studio and industrial processes including plaster lathes and jigger and jolly machines. We have recently introduced an option in experimental cast and kiln formed glass. We have our own kiln site in a rural area for Salt, Soda, Raku and all aspects of kiln building.

Hereford	**Herefordshire College of Art and Design** Folly Lane Hereford HR1 1LT Tel: (01432) 273359 Fax: (01432) 341099	**BA (Hons) Design Crafts:** Course prepares students for entrance into the professional world of the designer/maker. To achieve this objective the prerequisite skills and knowledge required for the successful running of a small business are directly reflected in the course philosophy, content and structure both at a practical and theoretical level. Options in: ceramics, metal, textiles. These are supported by a comprehensive range of media, both traditional and non-traditional. Technical material resource may be combined as appropriate. **City & Guilds of London Institute Creative Studies (7900)** Ceramics. This part-time one day a week course includes a wide range of forming and decorative techniques and is supported by visits to workshops, museums and galleries. Previous experience is not required and the programme is taught over two years with continuous assessment. A core unit 'preparing designs and working drawings' is included in the syllabus. Entry requirements minimum age 16 years. No formal qualifications. BTEC HNC part-time one day per week in Design Crafts with options in ceramics, textiles, metal. OCN units in Ceramics contributing to BTEC or other awards in Design Crafts.
High Wycombe	**Buckinghamshire College of Higher Education, a college of Brunel University** Queen Alexandra Road High Wycombe HP11 2JZ Tel: (01494) 522141 Fax: (01494) 524392	**BA (Hons) Ceramics with Glass** Applicants must have completed Art Foundation Course and be over 18 with 5 GCSEs or 3 GCSEs and one 'A' level. This exciting course provides a broad-based experience of working with both clay and glass, and students are taught both studio and industrial craft skills. The aim of the course is to help students develop a personal and visual awareness through working with these materials, thus providing a sound basis for their future development as artists and designers.
King's Lynn	**Norfolk College of Arts & Technology** Tennyson Avenue King's Lynn PE30 2Q Tel: (01553) 761144	**BTEC National Diploma in Ceramics** Two years full-time (part-time options available). A broad course covering all aspects of studio ceramics. Applications from mature students welcome.

Leicester	**School of Design and Manufacture De Montfort University** The Gateway Leicester LE1 9BH Tel: (0116) 2577545 Fax: (0116) 2506281	BA (Hons) Ceramics/Glass Entry requirements: 3 GCSEs inc. English, or equivalent plus 'A' levels, Foundation or The Gateway BTEC. Does accept direct entry. Applications from mature students welcome. Each student has the opportunity to work with a variety of media and experience a wide range of attitudes to problem solving. From the very beginning the course is involved with both the practice and theory of design for production as well as the realisation of personal dreams. Involvement in commercial and personal live projects, and a unique record in winning national competitions creates professional and proactive graduates. This is a modular pathway as part of BA (Hons) Three Dimensional Design programme. The university is using a compatible modular system thus allowing student choice and flexibility.
London	**Camberwell College of Arts** (The London Institute) Peckham Road London SE5 8U Tel: (0171) 514 6300 Fax: (0171) 514 6320	**BA (Hons) 3 Years Full-time.** This course interprets ceramics in its broadest sense, encouraging innovation and experimentation while retaining its specialist studio philosophy. Centred on practice-based study, it encourages students to explore the widest possibilities of this expressive medium, producing versatile makers and artists with a developed visual language. **Visual Arts BA Joint Honours** 3 years Full-time. Structure: The course allows students to study simultaneously two subjects from a choice of five areas. Possible options for ceramics are: Painting and printmaking; Sculpture; Electronic and Lens-based media; Graphic Design; Silversmithing and Metalwork. **Applied Arts MA** 1-year Full-time, 2-years Part-time. Camberwell is an internationally renowned centre for the applied arts, with a distinguished tradition of diverse activity, debate and innovation. The new MA in Applied Arts builds on this tradition and provides an opportunity for students of either Silversmithing and Metalwork or Ceramics to develop a strong theoretical position in relation to their continuing practice.
	Central Saint Martins College of Art & Design (The London Institute) Southampton Row London WC1B 4AP Tel: (0171) 753 9090 Fax: (0171) 242 0240	**BA (Hons) Ceramic Design** The course explores functional ceramic design through a wide range of approaches open to the ceramic designer. It produces graduates with a high level of intellectual maturity that makes them eligible for a number of distinctive careers open to the professional ceramist.

The City Lit
6 Bolt Court
off Fleet Street
London EC4A 3DQ
Tel: (0171) 405 2949
Fax: (0171) 585 7500

Ceramics Diploma. A two-year part-time (2 days per week) validated by London Guildhall University. A focus on contemporary ceramics offering a broad range of approaches and technique enabling students to set up own workshop or move to higher study. Ceramics is also included as an option in the BTEC Foundation course, and there are several structured courses in ceramics, day and evening.

(Greater London)

Barnet College
Wood Street
Barnet
Herts. EN5 4AZ
Tel: (0181) 440 6321
Fax: (0181) 441 5236

BTEC GNVQ Advanced in Art and Design Full-time 2-year diagnostic Art and Design 16+ **BTEC National Diploma in Design 3D Studies.** Full-time, wood, ceramics, engineering in application to product design.

West Herts College
Faculty of Visual
Communication
School of Art & Design
Callowland
Leavesden Road
Watford WD2 5EF
Tel: (01923) 221309
Fax: (01923) 225393

Diploma Part-time programme designed to encourage students with previous experience of ceramics to develop a personal approach with clay or follow a specific research pathway. Entry requirements: Students to have considerable experience of ceramic work, gained on vocational courses, experience of working potteries, or own ceramic work. The programme may also be of interest to recently graduated HND/BA students wishing to develop a body of work or research a particular area of ceramic technology.

City and Guilds of London Institute. Creative Studies Ceramics Part I Part-time 1 day a week course covering a range of making and decorative techniques to develop personal ways of working. Previous experience not required. 2-year course with continuous assessment. Creative Studies Ceramics Part II. For students who have completed Part I, this offers extended research study linked to design development and specific ceramic projects. Students may be able to progress from this programme to the Diploma Course. The school also offers an Access to Art & Design course. Students studying ceramics may combine with or progress to this programme.

University of Westminster
Harrow Campus
Northwick Park
Harrow HA1 3TP
Tel: (0171) 911 5000

3 year Workshop Ceramics BA (Hons)
Standard entry with Foundation or BTEC
Diploma. Non-standard entry for mature
students (21+). Geared to providing students
with all they require to be effective as
independent and collaborative practitioners, to
consider further studies, and to apply their
knowledge and judgment to related activities.
Provides frameworks for practical and
conceptual explorations of the fundamental
skills and technologies, including throwing,
handbuilding, glaze and body chemistry, the
construction, firing and analysis of kilns,
encourages material,critical and cultural
investigations of the artefact. Strongly focused
on creative evolution of the student's individual
practice. **MA Design & Media Arts** Half-year,
full or part-time, by project based on facilities
of several courses including ceramics.

West Thames College
London Road
Isleworth
Middlesex TW7 4HS
Tel: (0181) 568 0244
Fax: (0181) 569 7787

**BTEC Diploma in Foundation Art and Design
(including ceramics) 1 year.** Evening classes in
ceramics.

Loughborough

**Loughborough College of
Art & Design**
Radmoor
Loughborough
Leicester LE11 3BT
Tel: (01509) 261515
Fax: (01509) 265515

BA(Hons) 3-Dimensional Ceramics Entrance
qualifications as standard but main criteria for
acceptance is portfolio and commitment. As in
all Art and Design degrees 20% of the course is
taken up with academic work and prospective
students should be able to demonstrate an
ability to cope with the written work. The
course is a 3-year full-time (5-year part-time)
specialist degree in ceramics, there are support
studies in photography and computers in the
structured 1st year, and this leads progressively
into self-directed working in the 2nd and 3rd
years.

Lowestoft

**School of Art & Design
Lowestoft College**
St Peters Street
Lowestoft
Suffolk NR32 2N
Tel: (01502) 583521
Fax: (01502) 500031

BTEC HND in Ceramic Design/Studio Crafts
(subject to validation) 2 years full-time.
Requirements: Normally 4 GCSEs at Grade C or
above, or equivalent. However, if you are a
mature student, or if you can demonstrate
some prior knowledge of the subject or have a
good portfolio of general art-work which you
can present at interview, then we may be able
to accept you on to the course with fewer
formal qualifications. Practical experience
including drawing and visual research, surface
pattern design; studio crafts – handbuilding
and throwing; industrial ceramics; sculptural
ceramics; clay. glaze and kiln technologies;
mould-making and kiln building; business and
professional studies.

Manchester	**Manchester Metropolitan University** Faculty of Art and Design Department of Three Dimensional Design Chatham Building All Saints Manchester M15 6BR Tel: (0161) 247 1003	**BA (Hons) 3D Design, Wood, Metal, Ceramics, Glass.** This is a multi-disciplinary course where students may choose to specialise in ceramics during their final year. All students work across a wide area of materials. The course in ceramics covers all basic making techniques including throwing, handbuilding and simple mould making. A diverse range of approaches is encouraged in the expressive use of clay. The course is initially project-based and includes relevant glaze and kiln technology together with some historical studies. In the final year students develop their own personal approach to clay.
Middlesbrough and Hartlepool	**Cleveland College of Art and Design** Green Lane Middlesbrough Cleveland TS9 6DE Tel: (01642) 821441	**BTEC GNVQ and Foundation Studies** plus NCFE 'Access' course with specialisms in studio ceramics leading to advanced levels.
Nuneaton	**North Warwickshire and Hinckley College** Hinckley Road Nuneaton CV11 6BH Tel: (01203) 349321 Fax: (01203) 329056	**BTEC Higher National Diploma in 3D Design: Ceramics with Glass** 2 years full-time or 3 years part-time. Entry requirements normally 4 grade C or above, or BTEC National Diploma/Foundation course, or other relevant qualifications/experience. Most important is a portfolio of work demonstrating a commitment to ceramics, which forms the major part of this course with glass as an option. Applications particularly welcome from mature students. This course is run in partnership with the University of Central England in Birmingham, to which students may progress to obtain BA Hons. We cover as many making and finishing methods as possible, including throwing, handbuilding and industrial ceramics, plus history and technology and contextual studies. A practical course aimed to provide the designer/maker with sound experience and broad range of skills in ceramics. **BTEC National Diploma in Design: Ceramics.** 2 years full-time, or part-time by negotiation. Entry by 4 GCSEs, portfolio of work demonstrating enthusiasm for the subject, or other relevant experience. The course, designed for students interested in a professional career as designer/maker or technician, aims to provide students with the skills and knowledge necessary for continued education or for employment relating to their interests in the design studio or ceramic workshop.

Preston	**University of Central Lancashire** Faculty of Design and Technology Preston PR1 2HE (01772) 201201	**BA (Hons) Three Dimensional Design Course** Wood, Metal, Ceramics, Glass. The Course offers the opportunity to study three dimensional design work ranging from craft to design manufacture, and offers a broad range of disciplines which can be integrated or studied as specialist activities. We have a firm belief that the individuality of each student should be nurtured and that a multi-faceted course can produce graduates who have highly developed skills and are equipped for life as designer makers intending to satisfy exclusive markets or as designers for industry well versed in problem solving and product development. Course of Study: Initial study units introduce students to the knowledge and skills required for advanced study of specialist options, with projects becoming more student-initiated as the course progresses. With appropriate guidance students plot their own route through the programme.
Rochester	**Kent Institute of Art and Design** **Rochester-upon-Medway College** Fort Pitt Rochester Kent ME1 1DZ Tel: (01634) 830022 Fax: (01634) 829461	**BA Hons Ceramics** An integral part of the Three Dimensional Design course, the undergraduate programme offers a broad and divergent experience of ceramics investigating established processes and techniques of craft-based and industrial ceramics. Design projects which direct students' experience towards ceramics in Architecture, Public Art, within a Fine Art context or product design, will form a major part of 2nd year studies. **National Diploma in Design** Option in Ceramics, 2 years. Entry Requirements: Minimum age 16 years, minimum 3 GCSE/GCE 'O' levels or equivalent plus evidence of art/craft/design study. The course including drawing, painting and designing and complementary studies which encourages interest in the historical, social. economical and philosophical aspects of the craft. All techniques are covered.
Rotherham	**Rotherham College of Arts and Technology** Eastwood Lane Rotherham South Yorks S65 1EG Tel: (01709) 362111	**GCSE and City and Guilds courses** with options through the General Art and Design, Foundation and Access programmes, for people wishing to specialise in Ceramics through a higher education course.
Stafford	**Stafford College** Earl Street Stafford Staffordshire ST16 2QR Tel: (01785) 223800	**City and Guilds Creative Studies, Ceramics,** Ceramic Design and Production

Stoke-on-Trent	**Staffordshire University School of Design and Ceramics** Division of Ceramic Design College Road Stoke-on-Trent ST4 2DE Tel: (01782) 744531 Fax: (01782) 745627	**HND Design (Ceramics)** The course is of two years duration and offers a combination of creative, theoretical and practical learning. It is project based, supported by an extensive programme of practical skills, that include: three dimensional modelling and plaster work, print processes and ceramic manufacture. The course shares, with other ceramic courses, the finest ceramic facilities available in the UK. It has a very close relationship with the ceramic industry, which enables it to give students the benefit of a work placement which is usually in a design studio. **BA (Hons) Design (Ceramics)** This course offers a broadly based programme of study, where students initially acquire a wide range of specialist ceramic skills, before focusing on their chosen area of interest. The course shares, with our other ceramic courses the finest ceramic resources in the UK, this enables a diverse range of work to be produced which covers all aspects of ceramic practice.
Sunderland	**University of Sunderland** School of Arts, Design and Communications Ashbourne House Ryhope Road Sunderland SR2 7EF Tel: (0191) 5152123 Fax: (0191) 5152132 http://www.sunderland.ac.uk	**BA (Hons) 3D Design** (Glass, Architectural Glass and Ceramics) This programme has full-time and part-time modes and is a Modular Programme with Ceramics as a Core Study
Wolverhampton	**University of Wolverhampton** School of Art & Design Molineaux Street Wolverhampton WV1 1SB Tel: (01902) 321960 Fax: (01902) 321944	**MA or BA (Hons)** Ceramics may be studied on a full or part-time mode through specialist, major/minor, joint or triple joint programmes. The course covers all aspects of ceramic practice including studio or craft design, ceramic sculpture, figurative modelling, architectural and environmental clay work and ceramic product design using industrial techniques. The first year induction programme introduces students to all ceramic forming and technical processes. Following this students progressively define their future directions via tutor set and negotiated projects. Workshops and lectures frequently delivered by Subject staff and invited practitioners. Field trips are available throughout the year as well as opportunities to spend some time studying in Europe or North America.
WALES **Cardiff**	**University of Wales Institute, Cardiff** Howard Gardens Cardiff CF2 1SP Tel: (01222) 506618	**BA (Hons) Ceramics**

Carmarthen	**Carmarthenshire College of Technology & Art Faculty of Art & Design** Job's Well Road Carmarthen Dyfed SA31 3HY Tel: (01554) 759165 Ext. 72425	**HND Design Crafts** 2 years full-time course with specialist option in ceramics: studio, casting, handbuilding and modelling. Entry by N.D.D., G.A.D., Foundation or Access. Portfolio interview in each instance.
Newport	**University of Wales College Newport** College Crescent Caerleon Newport Gwent NP6 1XJ Tel: (01633) 430088 Fax: (01633) 432006	**BA Design Futures (validated by University of Wales BA (Hons) Graphics (validated by University of Wales)**
Wrexham	**NE Wales Institute of Higher Education** North Wales School of Art & Design 49 Regent Street Wrexham Clwyd LL11 1PF Tel: (01978) 290154	**BA (Hons) Design Ceramics** (3 year course) A modular structure with great emphasis placed on the enthusiasm and energy of the individual. Students who enjoy a challenge will encounter Workshop Activity, Architectural Ceramics, Glaze Technology, Visual Studies, Cultural, Historical and Contextual Studies. The course provides a thorough understanding of Ceramics in a theoretical and practical application. Students have opportunity to introduce other materials within their work, and are expected to take creative risks in an atmosphere of constructive criticism. A part-time course of study leading to this award is also available.
SCOTLAND Aberdeen	**Grays School of Art** The Robert Gordons University Garthdee Road Aberdeen AB9 2QD Tel: (01224) 263600	**BA (Hons) Design and Craft: 3D Design** Entry qualifications: 3 SCE 'H' incl. English + 2 ' O's or 2 GCE incl. English + 3 'O's. This specialism provides a foundation of knowledge and understanding to develop as a practitioner or team member in industry within the field of Ceramics, Product Design and Jewellery. Studies are underpinned by a common programme of drawing, CAD, Core Studies, Multi-Disciplinary Design and History of Design with Contextual Studies. This combination of specialist and generic skills is essential for designers/practitioners who will be committed to creating artefacts for the 21st Century.
Dundee	**University of Dundee Duncan of Jordanstone College of Art** School of Design Perth Road Dundee DD1 4HT Tel: (01382) 23261 Fax: (01382) 201378	**Degree Course Contemporary Ceramics B.Des (Hons)** 3 years. Normally 2 'A's + 3 'O' level passes or 3 SCE 'H's + 5 'O' grade passes. Foundation or General Art Diploma. Direct entry by interview.

Edinburgh	**Edinburgh College of Art** Heriot Watt University School of Design and Applied Arts Lauriston Place Edinburgh EH3 9DF Tel: (0131) 221 6128 Fax: (0131) 221 6004	**Degree Course/Ceramics BA (Hons)** 3 SCE 'H's incl.English , 2 SCE 'O's (C band or above). 2 GCE 'A's 3 GCE 'O's (including English at 'A' or 'O'). The Section aims to provide an input of manipulative skills and technical information running parallel to the development of each student's creative personality. Initially, set projects familiarise the students with a range of hand and machine processes applied to both form and surface design, great emphasis being placed on self-programming as the course develops. Clay, glaze and kiln theory and practice are thoroughly covered, and a programme of relevant historical studies is undertaken through lectures, museum visits and personal research.
Glasgow	**Glasgow School of Art** 167 Renfrew Street Glasgow G3 6RQ Tel: (0141) 353 4500	**(BA (Hons) BA Design** Academic requirements Scottish Certificate of Education – 3 Higher Grades (including English and Art) and any other 2 subjects at 'O' Grade, OR General Certificate of Education – 2 'A' levels (including Art and English) and 3 'O' levels. If 'A' level English not obtained, passes at 'O' level required in BOTH English literature and English language. OR equivalent qualifications including HNC, HND SCOTVEC, DATEC, BTEC and Higher English. Course principally involved in clay and plaster work, but students actively encouraged to experiment with a variety of materials and techniques.
NORTHERN IRELAND Belfast	**University of Ulster** Department of Fine and Applied Arts York Street Belfast BT15 1ED Tel: (01232) 328515 Fax: (01232) 267310 http://www.ulst.ac.uk	**DipHE/BA Hons Fine & Applied Arts** Study Areas: Ceramics; Silversmithing and Jewellery; Embroidery/Textile Art; Printing; Sculpture; Lens-based media; History and Theory. This module-based course provides students with the opportunity to specialize early or to take a broader pathway through a range of study areas. At the end of the third year of study students will be awarded BA Hons. Exceptionally students may be awarded a DipHE award instead at the end of the second year.

Post Graduate Courses in Ceramics

Aberdeen

Grays School of Art
The Robert Gordons
University
Garthdee Road
Aberdeen AB9 2QD
Tel: (01224) 313247

Post Graduate Diploma Ceramics 1 year Post Graduate Diploma; BA (CNAA) or equivalent.

Belfast

University of Ulster
Department of Fine and
Applied Arts
York Street
Belfast BT15 1ED
Tel: (01232) 328515
Fax: (01232) 267310
http://www.ulst.ac.uk

Postgraduate Certificate/Diploma/MA Applied Arts This is a module-based course which may be undertaken in the following ways: 2 years Full-time: 1st year; 1st semester to Certificate, 2nd semester to Diploma. 2nd year; 2 semesters to MA. 3/4 years Part-time: 1st year, 2 semesters to Certificate, 2nd year; 2 semesters to Diploma, 3rd/4th year 3 semesters to MA. Application is by proposal and any range of appropriate study area will be considered. European Social Fund Awards may be available in the 2nd year of course.

Cardiff

University of Wales Institute, Cardiff
Howard Gardens
Cardiff CF2 1SP
Tel: (01222) 506615

MA Ceramics

Dundee

University of Dundee
Duncan of Jordanstone
College of Art
School of Design
Perth Road
Dundee DD1 4HT
Tel: (01382) 23261
Fax: (01382) 201378

One year postgraduate M.Des. By interview with good degree 1st or 2:1. September start.

Edinburgh

Edinburgh College of Art
Heriot Watt University
School of Design and
Applied Arts
Lauriston Place
Edinburgh EH3 9DF
Tel: (0131) 221 6128
Fax: (0131) 221 6004

Postgraduate Diploma in Design (one academic year). Master of Design (MDES) (15 months) MPHIL and PHD. The postgraduate programmes provide a focused period of study intended to develop a candidate's independent thinking, creative ideas and skills in problem solving, while extending experience in the handling of relevant materials and processes. Candidates for higher degrees are expected to extend specific areas of knowledge in their department while making a contribution to its vitality and richness, both through the originality of their own practical work and through assisting in agreed aspects of the undergraduate course input.

Glasgow

Glasgow School of Art
167 Renfrew Street
Glasgow G3 6RQ
Tel: (0141) 353 4500

4-Term Masters in Design September-December following year.

London	**Middlesex University** Cat Hill Barnet Herts. EN4 8HTMA Tel: (0181) 362 5000 Fax: (0181) 440 9541	**Post Graduate Level** 1 year full-time or 2 years part-time MA Art and Design MA Design.
	Royal College of Art Kensington Gore London SW7 2EU Tel: (0171) 590 4444 Fax: (0171) 590 4500	**MA/M.Phil/PhD** Ceramics & Glass 2-year courses in Designing and making Ceramics and Glass, Architectural Decoration, Design for Ceramics and Glass Industry. Research Projects in Ceramics and Glass. Materials and Technology. Entry requirements: a first degree or the equivalent experience. Competitive entrance examination February/March each year.
(Greater London)	**West Herts College** Faculty of Visual Communication School of Art & Design Callowland Leavesden Road Watford WD2 5EF Tel: (01923) 221309 Fax: (01923) 225393	**Postgraduate/Experience Diploma** in Ceramics (Subject to Validation).
Rochester	**Kent Institute of Art & Design** Rochester-upon-Medway College Fort Pitt Rochester Kent ME1 1DZ Tel: (01634) 830022 Fax: (01634) 829461	**MA Ceramics** Graduates are encouraged to develop an in depth understanding of ceramic practice within a three dimensional design context. Postgraduate study will seek to explore and challenge the boundaries between art, craft and design through both core programme of lectures and seminars, and a personal project.
Stoke-on-Trent	**Staffordshire University** School of Design and Ceramics Division of Ceramic Design College Road Stoke-on-Trent ST4 2DE Tel: (01782) 744531 Fax: (01782) 745637	**Postgraduate Diploma/MA Design (Ceramics)** This linked programme of courses is primarily concerned with ceramic design for small and mass manufacture. The programme offers a one-year (34 weeks) postgraduate diploma with the opportunity for progression to either MA full-time or MA sandwich. The full-time route requires in total 53 weeks of continuous study. The sandwich route requires in total two years of full-time study which includes an industrial placement at the beginning of the second year.

Craft Potters Association 1995-97 Contemporary Ceramics

Exhibitions

1995
Clayworks IV: CPA Associate Members   (January)
New Members Show: Peter Clough, John Higgins, Ashley Howard, Joanna Howells, Anne James, Marcio Mattos, Aki Moriuchi, Will Marshall   (March)
Ian Gregory: New Work   (May)
Ruthanne Tudball: New Work   (June)
Colin Pearson: New Work   (July)
Setting Out: Selected Art School Graduates   (August)
Duncan Ross: New Work   (October)
Christmas Glitter: (November)

1996
Fireworks 3:   Craft Potters Association Professional Members   (January)
Salt & Soda: Sheila Casson, Jack Doherty, Jane Hamlyn, Peter Meanley, Walter Keeler, Phil Rogers, Micki Schloessingk, Ruthanne Tudball, Sarah Walton   (March)
Phil Rogers: New Work   (May)
Nigel Lambert: New Work   (June)
Setting Out: Selected Art School Graduates   (August)
Jim Malone: New Work   (September)
Peter Lane: New Work   (October)

1997
V & A Prizewinners: Stefanie Dinkelbach, Susan Halls, Emma Rodgers, Helen Talbot   (February)
Gala Re-opening of Contemporary Ceramics with Guests of Honour Una Stubbs and Tony Ford, Director of the Crafts Council   (May)
Kaleidoscope: A changing exhibition to celebrate the opening of the newly refurbished shop and gallery   (May)
Emily Myers: New Work   (June)

Events and Meetings 1995-97
Organised by the Members and Associates Advisory Committee

1995
Geoffrey Eastop – Visit to his pottery at Ecchinswell, Berkshire   (January)
Elspeth Owen – Lecture/Slides /Video 'Personal Work and Ideas'. The Museum of Mankind, London   (April)
Michael Casson – Lecture/Slides 'Fifty Years of Making Pots: A Personal View'. Linean Society, London   (May)
AGM with Jane Perryman – Talk/Slides 'Traditional Indian Pottery'. Quaker Meeting House, London   (June)
Nigel Barley – Lecture and guided tour of 'Smashing Pots' exhibition of African pottery. Museum of Mankind, London   (September)

Josie Walter and David Roberts – Slides/Demonstrations on their individual approaches to clay handling and surface treatments. Long Road 6th Form College, Cambridge   (October)

Talk by Amanda Fielding, Curator of The Crafts Collection showing selection of contemporary ceramics from the Crafts Council's Collection. Open Meeting, Crafts Council, London   (October)

Phil Rogers and Peter Beard – Lecture/Slides 'Project Ploughshare' the scheme to assist Ethiopian women potters. Museum of Mankind, London   (November)

Christmas Presence Pottery Festival – Slide Lectures/ Discussions with Michael Casson and Jack Troy   (December)

1996

Open Meeting at Crafts Council – Morris Latham, Head of Sales Development on looking at ways of selling. Crafts Council, London   (January)

Guided Tour by Shelagh Vainker of Eastern Art Departments of Chinese, Japanese and Islamic Ceramics. Ashmolean Museum, Oxford   (February)

Visit to Winchcombe Pottery hosted by Mike and Ray Finch   (April)

Jill Crowley – Lecture/Slides 'Exploring Raku Fired Figurative Ceramics'. Linnean Society, London   (May)

Guided Tour of Victoria & Albert Museum's Far Eastern Department   (June)

Earth and Fire II – Ceramics Fair at Rufford Country Park   (July)

'What's Brewing' Exhibition of Teapots, Coffee Pots at The Art Connoisseur Gallery, London   (August)

Earth and Fire II – Ceramics Fair at Rufford Country Park   (July)

Visit to Ian Gregory's Workshop, Dorset   (September)

Alison Britton – Lecture/Slides 'Form and Fiction' Linnean Society, London (November)

1997

Walter Keeler – Two Slide Lectures 'The Story of My Life' and 'A History of Saltglaze' Joint CPA/East Anglian Potters Event. Long Road 6th Form College, Cambridge   (February)

Study Session 'Staffordshire Slipware 1670-1750' and 'Staffordshire Saltglaze Stoneware 1730-1780' with Kathy Niblett, Senior Assistant Keeper of Ceramics and Eileen Hampson, Author and Collector. Stoke-on-Trent City Museum   (March)

Kiln Building demonstrated by Ben Casson. Open Meeting The Royal Forest of Dean College, Gloucestershire   (May)

Matthias Ostermann – Slide Lecture 'Maiolica: Surface Decoration, A Contemporary Approach' St Paul's School, London   (May)

Craft Potters Association of Great Britain Ltd.

Council 1996

Chair
Vice-Chair
Hon. Secretary

Jack Doherty
Gaynor Lindsell
Liz Gale
Emmanuel Cooper, Margaret Frith,
Ashley Howard, John Jelfs, Eileen
Lewenstein, John Wheeldon

Associate Representative	Elizabeth Smith
CPA News Representative	Chris Speyer
Accounts	Jan Abel

Contemporary Ceramics
Craft Potters Shop and Gallery

Manager	Marta Donaghey
Assistants	Johanna Bergmann, Clare Dixon, Lucy Howard

Ceramic Review

Editors	Eileen Lewenstein, Emmanuel Cooper
Sub-Editor	Julia Pitts
Editorial Assistant, Advertising	Daphne Matthews
Subscriptions and Books	Marilyn Kopkin
Assistant (CPA & Shop)	Daniel Stanley

Useful Addresses

Ceramic Review
21 Carnaby Street
London
W1V 1PH

Craft Potters Association
21 Carnaby Street
London W1V 1PH

Crafts Council
44a Pentonville Road
London
N1 9BY

Contemporary Applied Arts
2 Percy Street
London W1P 9FA

Arts Council
14 Great Peter Street
London SW1P 3NQ

Welsh Design Advisory Service
Cardiff Institute of H.E.
Western Avenue
Cardiff CF5 2YD

Design Directorate
Netherleigh Massey Avenue
Belfast EH3 7DD

Welsh Arts Council
Holst House
9 Museum Place
Cardiff CF1 3NX

Scottish Arts Council
12 Manor Place
Edinburgh EH3 7DD

Rural Development Commission
141 Castle Street
Wiltshire SP1 3TP

Regional Arts Boards

North West Arts
Manchester House
22 Bridge Street
Manchester M3 3AB

South East Arts
10 Mount Ephraim
Tunbridge Wells
TN4 8AS

Eastern Arts
Cherry Hinton Hall
Cambridge CB1 4DW

East Midlands Arts
Epinal Way
Loughborough
LE11 0QE

London Arts
Elme House
133 Long Acre
London WC2E 9AF

Northern Arts
10 Osborne Terrace
Newcastle-upon-Tyne NE2 1NZ

Southern Arts
13 St. Clement Street
Winchester SO23 3DQ

South West Arts
Bradninch Place
Gandy Street
Exeter EX4 3LS

West Midlands Arts
82 Granville Street
Birmingham
B1 2LH

Yorkshire & Humberside Arts
21 Bond Street
Dewsbury WF13 1AX

CONTEMPORARY
CERAMICS

CRAFT POTTERS SHOP AND GALLERY

POTS   BOOKS   TOOLS   EXHIBITIONS

CONTEMPORARY
CERAMICS

7 Marshall Street, London W1V 1LP
OPEN MONDAY - SATURDAY 10-5.30pm THURSDAY 10-7PM
TELEPHONE   0171-437   7605

LOCATION MAP

This map gives approximate geographical locations for potters with workshops open to the public. Map numbers correspond to those proceeding the names and addresses (see page 288). It is advisable to telephone individuals prior to making a special journey.

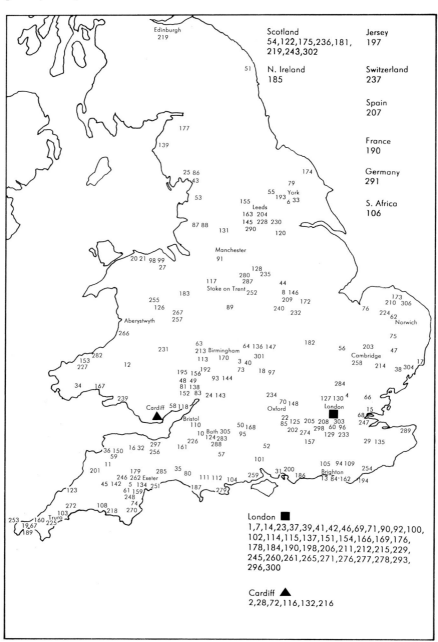